LECTURES

ON THE

DOCTRINE OF ELECTION.

BY

ALEXANDER C. RUTHERFORD,

MINISTER OF THE GOSPEL, GREENOCK.

PHILADELPHIA:

HIGGINS & PERKINPINE,

40 NORTH FOURTH STREET.

1854.

E. B. MEARS, STEREOTYPER.

MERRIHEW & THOMPSON, PRINTERS.

PHILADELPHIA, Feb. 25, 1854.

Messrs. HIGGINS & PERKINPINE,—

I have read with some care the "Lectures on Election, by the Rev. Alexander C. Rutherford, of Greenock," and I consider the work to be an able exposition of the errors of the predestinarian theory, by one who has had every opportunity of understanding that theory, as held by its ablest advocates. The argument is clear and convincing; and, for general circulation, I deem this book one of the best on the subject with which it has been my fortune to meet.

GEO. R. CROOKS, M. A.

PHILADELPHIA, January 4, 1854.

Messrs. HIGGINS & PERKINPINE,—

I have read a work entitled "Lectures on the Doctrine of Election, by Alexander C. Rutherford, Minister of the Gospel, Greenock," and while I am not prepared to subscribe to all its minor positions, nor to justify all its severities of expression, many of which were prompted, I suppose, by circumstances not apparent to the reader, I unhesitatingly recommend it as an unanswerable refutation of the Calvinistic doctrines of election and reprobation, as placing the truth in a very clear and convincing light, and as eminently worthy to be republished and widely circulated, especially in view of the efforts now made to engage the public confidence for the unscriptural and dangerous tenets which it condemns.

FRANCIS HODGSON, D. D.

PREFACE.

The following Discourses were originally delivered in Greenock, towards the close of last year, and were again delivered in Glasgow in consequence of a requisition, numerously subscribed, by Christian brethren in that city. They were not prepared with any intention of publication, and their publication has been acquiesced in by the author in deference to the request of those who heard them from the pulpit. It is hoped that, in spite of all their imperfections, they may perhaps do good. They have already opened the eyes of many former opponents who heard them delivered. It will be observed that a few remarks have been appended to some of the Lectures, chiefly of a practical kind, and here and there a few sentences have been added to, or subtracted from, the original manuscript. This was deemed necessary as each Lecture was necessarily prepared rather hurriedly and formed one of three discourses preached weekly to a kind and indulgent people. The author is no advocate in general for three discourses being extorted from any minister each successive Sabbath, but there are exceptions to every general rule; and the present position of the cause with which he has the privilege to be connected, induces the necessity for more abundant labour upon brethren in the ministry. When he was a minister in the United Secession (now United Presbyterian) Church, the author was wont to think that Sabbath evening sermons, in addition to other work, was a cunning device of Satan, for the purpose of killing the clergy. He thinks so still. On this point he is quite orthodox in sentiment. It is a remarkable circumstance however, that so long as the author was orthodox upon other points he never found it either necessary or expedient regularly to trespass in his labour beyond the ordinary canonical hours of public Sabbath-day worship, *i. e.*, forenoon and afternoon. It would perhaps be too sweeping and hasty an inference to conclude from this simple fact, that Satan has a particular liking for modern orthodoxy. Such would be a very hasty conclusion to draw from one solitary fact, assuming that fact to be correct, and withal it would be vastly uncharitable to include our ancient orthodox friends in an alliance with the wicked one, unless the fact of such an alliance can be clearly demonstrated. If, however, such a demonstration be possible, then it ceases to be uncharitable to exhibit it, and thus to warn our esteemed brethren of their position and their danger. In this case, brotherly love and ancient friendship and affection, demands the production of the evidence which would demonstrate, beyond the possibility of refutation, that, under the banner of truth, our orthodox brethren are really, though undesignedly, engaged in the support and propagation of deadly error. Such is the evidence which we profess to exhibit in the following Lectures. It is for the reader to say, after a candid and prayerful examination of the evidence, whether or not it amounts to a satisfactory demonstration. If it do not, we know enough of our former brethren, to assert that there is among them, more especially in this good town of Greenock, plenty of orthodox zeal, and plenty of talent and learning, to enable them to point out our mistake. We respectfully invite them to the task, and we pledge ourselves PUBLICLY TO RECANT our error, the moment it is pointed out; and most cordially to thank the brother who shall take the trouble to prove us in the wrong. Should our Calvinistic friends resort to their ordinary mode of warfare, it will not be expected that we should follow them into the region of declamation or personal abuse. Of this we are contented to take our share, in the company of better men, who have preceded us in the advocacy of gospel truth against Calvinistic error. Of such abuse we have many examples in the writings of the great champion of Calvinism, AUGUSTUS TOPLADY, to whom reference is made in the following Lectures.

This writer is pleased to conclude his preface to Zanchius on Predestination, with the following reference to a man of whom the world was not worthy—

John Wesley—with the quotation of which we beg to close our prefatory remarks.

"Here ended [says Toplady] the first lesson: *i. e.*, here ended the preface to the former edition of this tract,—a tract, whose publication has raised the indignant quills of more than one Arminian porcupine.

"Among those enraged porcupines, none has, hitherto, bristled up so fiercely as the high and mighty *Mr. John Wesley.* He even dipt his quills in the ink of forgery, on the occasion; as Indians tinge the points of their arrows with poison, in hope of their doing more effectual execution. The quills, however, have reverberated, and with ample interest, on poor *Mr. John's* own pate. He *felt* the unexpected pain, and he has *squeaked* accordingly. I will not here add to the well-deserved chastisement he has received; which, from more than one quarter, has been such as will probably keep him *sore*, while his surname begins with W. Let him, for his own sake, learn, as becomes a very *sore* man, to *lie still.* Rest may do him good: motion will but add to his fever, by irritating his humours, already too peccant. Predestination is a *stone*, by rashly falling on which he has, more than once, been lamentably *broken.* I wish him to take heed, in due season, lest that stone at length fall on him. For notwithstanding all his delinquencies, I would still have him avoid, if possible, the catastrophe of being *ground to powder.*"

Greenock, 68, Union Street,
June, 1848.

CONTENTS.

THEORY FIRST, OR ELECTION TO A SPECIAL AND EXCLUSIVE INTEREST IN THE DEATH OF CHRIST; BEING THE ULTRA-CALVINISTIC THEORY.

LECTURE FIRST.

LECTURE SECOND.

PAGE

LECTURE THIRD.

LECTURE FOURTH.

THEORY SECOND, OR ELECTION TO A SPECIAL AND EXCLUSIVE INTEREST IN THE WORK OF THE SPIRIT; BEING THE MODERATE CALVINISTIC THEORY.

LECTURE FIFTH.

PAGE

LECTURE SIXTH.

LECTURE SEVENTH.

LECTURE EIGHTH.

THEORY THIRD, OR THE BIBLE DOCTRINE OF ELECTION EXHIBITED.

LECTURE NINTH.

LECTURE NINTH *continued.*

APPENDIX.

THE DOCTRINE OF ELECTION.

LECTURE FIRST.

ELECTION SHORTLY DEFINED—SHOULD BE CANDIDLY EXAMINED—INVOLVES REPROBATION—ULTRA-CALVINISTIC THEORY STATED—QUOTATION FROM JOHN CALVIN—FROM DR. R. CANDLISH—CONSISTENCY OF CANDLISH WITH THE CONFESSION—THIS THEORY THE SOURCE OF A FALSE AND DANGEROUS PEACE—IT CONTRADICTS AND SUBVERTS THE GOSPEL—WHAT IS THE GOSPEL?

ROM. viii. 33.—"Who shall lay anything to the charge of God's elect?"

EPH. ii. 3.—"In times past, ... we were by nature the children of wrath, even as others."

MARK, xvi. 15.—"Go ye into all the world, and preach the gospel to every creature."

THE two passages of Scripture which have first been read, refer to the same individuals at different stages of their spiritual history. These individuals are styled "God's elect," and they are referred to very frequently in the Word of God, more especially in the New Testament writings. The same idea which is couched under the term "elect," is more simply expressed by the word "chosen." Hence we have the statement made respecting the individuals referred to, that God the Father "hath chosen" them—a statement which occurs in various passages of the apostolic epistles. The choice referred to in one and all of the passages of Scripture in which the term occurs, is the choice of God, and this choice is called by the name of ELECTION. Election, then, may be shortly defined, as God's choice, or selection, of certain individuals of the human family, to the possession of eternal life. That God does, in point of fact, exercise such a choice,—that he does make such a selection,—is a plainly revealed, a well accredited doctrine of Scripture. There never did exist, and there does not at the present day exist, any difference of sentiment upon this fundamental point, among those who are agreed in the recognition of the Scriptures of the Old and New Testaments, as the infallible word of the infallible Jehovah. About this, there is no debate whatever among professing Christians. And it is well that, in the very outset of our inquiry into this momentous subject, we should be privileged to meet each other upon common ground, and to give each other the right hand of fellowship, over the recognition of the blessed Bible as the Word of God, and the farther recognition of the great fundamental principle, that in the salvation of sinners God does exercise a free and sovereign choice. Here, then, we are all of one mind, and we may here most appropriately breathe forth the united and heartfelt prayer, that we may every one of us be guided in our investigations by the Holy Spirit, so that we may have grace to act consistently with our common profession.

Let the Word of God be recognised as the sole and exclusive arbiter in every matter of debate. Let the opinions of wise men and good men, which we shall have occasion freely and frequently to examine, be brought to the test of Scripture; and by that only infallible standard of truth, let them be received, or let them be rejected. Let it not be for one moment imagined, that any mere man is entitled to the credit of infallibility; and far less let it be supposed that in freely and strongly disapproving of the sentiments of any man, or any body of men, we are thereby treating them with any measure of disrespect, or cherishing for our fellow Christians from whom we may differ in sentiment, any feeling different from that of Christian affection and esteem. Let it be our aim, my brethren, to carry with us into this investigation which lies before us, the spirit and the bearing of a free and enlightened Christianity; and let me express the hope, that you will, one and all of you, candidly and carefully examine what may be set before you from this place, and compare it with the Word of God, and receive it, or reject it, as you may be satisfied from examination, that it agrees with or differs from that infallible record. Finally, here, let me remind myself, and remind you, of the apostolic and appropriate injunction, "Laying aside all malice, and all guile, and hypocrisies, and envies, and all evil speakings, as new-born babes, desire the sincere milk of the word, that ye may grow thereby" (1 Peter ii. 1, 2).

In examining the doctrine of Election, we shall include, in our investigation, the kindred doctrine of

Reprobation. It is impossible indeed to look at the one doctrine without at the same time recognising the other. They are not so much different doctrines as two different aspects of one and the same truth. The one involves the other by necessity of nature. The idea of choosing some, implies the idea of rejecting others. And though it be a truth, that some writers upon the doctrine make an attempt to separate and divide, so as to hold the doctrine of election without admitting the opposite doctrine of reprobation, it is most evident that they are here not more opposed to common sense and Scripture declaration, than they are to John Calvin himself. In the twenty-third chapter of the third book of his Institutes, Calvin thus expresses himself upon this subject: "Many indeed, as though they would drive away the malice from God, do so grant election, that they deny that any man is reprobated; but this they do too ignorantly and childishly: forasmuch as election itself could not stand unless it were set contrary to reprobation; therefore whom God passeth over he rejecteth; and for no other cause, but for that he will exclude them from the inheritance which he doth predestinate to be his children's." Such is the statement of the great founder of the system which goes by his name. And we do not see how it is possible for any man to admit, that God makes a selection of some men from the corrupt mass of humanity, without implying by this admission, that God rejects, by the same act, the rest of mankind, and thereby consigns them to misery. It is not as if the Deity were possessed of mere finite intelligence. It is not as if his omniscience could not, and did not, take in at a single glance, the entire generations of mankind. It is not as if he were in some danger of overlooking a great proportion of his creatures, so that while he chooses some, he might possibly pass by the others, without any definite or well-ordered design. We submit it as an axiom which may not be disputed, that the great God does nothing ignorantly nor rashly;—that whatever God does in time, he purposed from eternity to do;—and therefore, while we might say of ignorant and short-sighted man, that his choice of any given object does not necessarily involve a deliberate and final rejection of any other object, which may be placed at his disposal, we cannot hazard such an assertion, respecting the omniscient and all-wise Jehovah. Short-sighted and fallible mortals may, and do exercise the power of choice in reference to many things, without any knowledge whatever of, or any mental reference to, other objects which lie before them. They may, in other words, choose or select, most ignorantly and most rashly. But this will not be said of God. And therefore it ought at once to be admitted, that whatever proves and establishes any given theory of election, necessarily proves and establishes the corresponding theory of reprobation, so that the one must, according to the statement of Calvin himself, stand or fall with the other, and so, that unless a man be prepared to face up in the bold defence of reprobation, he ought to give his theory of election to the winds, and turn it adrift as a useless thing.

What then are the conflicting theories or doctrines

of election and reprobation which severally claim the reception of men?

There is, in the first place, that theory which affirms that the whole human race come into existence, some of them necessarily and irreversibly destined to eternal life—and others of them, necessarily and irreversibly bound over to eternal punishment, without any reference whatever to their voluntary reception of salvation on the one hand, or their voluntary rejection of it on the other. Some infants are born into the world without any possibility of coming short of eternal felicity. Other infants come into existence without any possibility of escaping eternal damnation. And so, men and women come into being, and grow up under the government of God, simply and exclusively to meet their separate and their final destinies. The elect are born into the world, possessed of all the privileges, and entitled to all the blessings, of the children of God, seeing that for them only, the Son of God shed his blood upon the cross. The reprobate come into existence under the curse, which cannot possibly be removed, and which has not been removed, seeing that Jesus did not become a curse for them. In reference to the one class, it may be said that their salvation is unalterably certain, and their perdition as impossible as it is to pull down Jesus from his mediatorial throne. In reference to all the rest of the human race, it may be said, that their damnation is certain, so that it is as sure that they shall perish eternally as that the devils are reserved in chains against the judgment of the great day.

Such is the commonly received doctrine of election on the one hand, and of reprobation on the other. This is called the Calvinistic theory, because its great originator and patron saint is John Calvin of renowned memory; and such is the doctrine which comes first before us for examination. It goes under the general name of predestination, and it is briefly stated by Calvin in the following words, which we quote from section fifth of the twenty-first chapter of the third book of his Institutes:—

"Predestination we call the eternal decree of God, whereby he had it determined with himself what he willed to become of every man. For all men are not created to like estate: but to some eternal life and to some eternal damnation is fore-appointed."

We crave your especial attention to the emphatic words, "All men are not created to like estate,"—implying, as they do imply, the strange idea, that some are created,—brought into existence,—for the express and definite purpose of damnation, and for no other end whatever. And lest any one should imagine that these words, which we have quoted from Calvin's writings, embody a sentiment which is now exploded and departed from, permit me here to add a quotation from the celebrated Dr. Robert Candlish of Edinburgh. I quote from page seventh of the doctor's book upon the Atonement,—a book which is universally commended by Calvinistic divines. Speaking of the work of the Son of God, this writer says—

"In right of his merit, his service, and his sacrifice, all are given into his hands, and all are his. All, therefore, may be said to be bought by him, inasmuch as, by his humiliation, obedience, and death, he has obtained, as by purchase, a right over all—he has got all under his power. But it is for very different purposes and ends. The reprobate are his to be judged; the elect are his to be saved. As to the former, it is no ransom, or redemption, fairly so called. He has won them—bought them, if you will—but it is that he may so dispose of them, as to glorify the retributive righteousness of God in their condemnation."

So you will observe that this eminent and influential writer expresses, most clearly and distinctly, the idea which Calvin brings out in the memorable words already quoted—"All men are not created to like estate." They are brought into existence "for very different purposes and ends." The tender-hearted mother, as she nurses the infant at her breast, and meanwhile listens to the innocent prattle of her first-born as he gambols playfully by her side, is here taught, that in all likelihood, these two children have been brought into being for "very different purposes and ends." And when she would prayerfully commit them both to Christ, and rejoice in the thought that the precious blood of the Lamb of God was shed for them, as well as for herself, she is told that though it be true that Christ "has bought" them both, it may very possibly be "for very different purposes and ends." The younger child may, for aught she knows, belong to Christ, only that Jesus may acquire the right over that inoffensive babe to condemn it through eternity; while the elder may, by a possibility, be purchased for a nobler destiny. One thing is certain, that as "all men are not created to like estate," and as no atonement has been made for any save the elect, should these interesting children not chance to be among the chosen number, the mother must make up her mind to thank God for bringing them into existence, the heirs of eternal damnation, and handing them over to his Son, not that his Son may die for their sins, but that he may consign them to a far more aggravated, and still more tremendous condemnation, than if he never had died at all.

Let no one turn round upon the eminent and distinguished man from whom I have quoted such sentiments, and impute any measure of blame to him, as if he were thereby writing inconsistently with the Confession which the people who support him compel him in honesty to teach. The people of every Calvinistic church, who do not relish such sentiments, have no right or title whatever to complain of their clergy for inculcating them. Every man who throws his influence into the scale of a Calvinistic church, thereby adds his weight and influence in the support and perpetuation of the doctrine I have now stated, be it right, or be it wrong. And God forbid that we should quote such sentiments for the purpose of pandering to, or in any way excusing, the inconsistencies of those who are prepared at once to start back from such sentiments, and who nevertheless support their ministers, for the express purpose of teaching them and perpetuating them, in full force, in the land. The sentiments I have quoted, are the sentiments of an honourable and upright man, who consistently expresses, in the quotation I have made, the doctrine of the Confession of Faith, which the people of Scotland, by their adherence to that Confession, compel their ministers to teach.

That there may exist no mistake upon this subject, let me here quote from that venerable Confession. The third chapter of that document contains the following words :—

"(3.) By the decree of God, for the manifestation of his glory, some men and angels are predestinated unto everlasting life, and others foreordained to everlasting death.

"(4.) These angels and men, thus predestinated and foreordained, are particularly and unchangeably designed; and their number is so certain and definite, that it cannot be either increased or diminished.

"(5.) Those of mankind that are predestinated unto life, God, before the foundation of the world was laid, according to his eternal and immutable purpose, and the secret counsel and good pleasure of his will, hath chosen in Christ unto everlasting glory, out of his mere free grace and love, without any foresight of faith or good works, or perseverance in either of them, or any other thing in the creature, as conditions, or causes moving him thereunto; and all to the praise of his glorious grace.

"(6.) As God hath appointed the elect unto glory, so hath he, by the eternal and most free purpose of his

I have quoted enough to serve my purpose, in the present discourse. My design is, to set before your minds a clear and distinct statement of the theory which we have engaged to examine. I wish you to know what that doctrine really is, and to satisfy yourselves, not from my statements merely, but from the published statements of Calvinists themselves, of the real merits of the system which is all but universally received,—the system in which the children of our native land are trained up from their infancy, and to oppose or speak against which, is the most outrageous heresy. Do not forget, then, I pray you, what I have now read from the Confession of Faith. We are informed, in the passage last quoted, that every soul of men who is destined to perdition, if God so willed it, might be saved. This is not a mere inference; it is a direct and explicit assertion, for the passage speaks of God withholding his grace, whereby the men, who are destined to hell fire, "might have been enlightened in their understandings, and wrought upon in their hearts." These words are sufficiently plain and definite. The poor men "might have been enlightened" and "wrought upon"—they might easily have been saved—but they are deprived, by the God who made them, of the very thing which alone was needful to win them over to his service, and place them secure in a position of holiness and happiness for ever. Let this statement of the Confession of Faith be marked down by every man and woman in this assembly. But there is more than this to mark down and to remember. We are informed, that God Almighty exerts his power for the purpose of entrapping the men into positive iniquity. What is it, my friends, that is ascribed to our God? He is said not only to withhold what would make men saints, "but" (it is expressly added) "sometimes" he "withdraweth the gifts which they had, and exposeth them to such objects as their corruption makes occasion of sin; and withal, gives them over to their own lusts, the temptations of the world, and the power of Satan." This is what our holy heavenly Father is said to do, in order to insure the fulfilment of his purposes and decrees. Again we call upon you to mark, that it is not by a simple negation—a mere refusal to give to the reprobate who perish what it is said would be enough to save them—it is more than this. It is by an actual, a positive, a direct act of his omnipotence, that God is represented as insuring the damnation of his creatures. They had gifts, but these gifts God withdraweth from them, lest they should happily repent, and before they die, use such gifts for their salvation. They were not in the way of sinning with a high hand, but we are told, by this most orthodox Confession, that God takes special care to expose them to such objects as will infallibly awaken their corruption and insure their fall. And, as if it were not enough to give them over to their own lusts, and expose them to such worldly temptations as God knows will infallibly master them, God is exhibited, as handing them over to the power of Satan, in order to make assurance doubly sure, and thereby the more readily secure their ultimate perdition.

The statements which have been quoted will suffice as an exhibition of the doctrine which we are engaged now in examining. Such quotations might easily be multiplied from the published writings of sound and orthodox Calvinists, some of which, it many not be unnecessary to refer to in the course of farther examination. Meanwhile, it is high time for us to pass from the statement of what the doctrine is, to an examination of the Scriptural grounds upon which we think it ought to be rejected.

I.—WE OBJECT, IN THE FIRST PLACE, THEN, TO THIS THEORY OF ELECTION, BECAUSE IT LEADS UNCONVERTED SINNERS TO SUPPOSE THAT VERY POSSIBLY THEY MAY BE SAFE ENOUGH EVEN IN THEIR UNBELIEF.

The words which are contained in the first of those two texts, to which we have referred you in the outset of this discourse, are very plain and explicit. The challenge is boldly made—"Who shall lay anything to the charge of God's elect?" And it is, as if the apostle had said, that it is impossible to lay anything to their charge. They are justified by God himself, and no being in the universe of God may venture to condemn them. Such is the entire strain of the apostle's unanswerable reasoning in the eighth chapter of the Romans, where the passage referred to occurs. It is perfectly plain, therefore, at the very first glance of this text, that the elect of God, whoever they are and wherever they be, are safe. They are secure as in a munition of adamantine rock. "It is God that justifieth; who is he that condemneth?" But the other passage, which we have asked you to turn up in the second chapter of the Epistle to the Ephesians, states most plainly, that the elect of God, to whom the apostle wrote, and among whom Paul included himself, were not always safe. They were not always in a position in which it could be said of them, "Who can lay anything to their charge?" They were once condemned. They were once the children of wrath even as others. They were once in precisely the same position in the sight of God, if not in the sight of men, which is occupied by every one of the rebellious generations of mankind. There was no difference whatever between them and the reprobate, and if they had died while they were yet the children of wrath, they must have endured the wrath of God throughout a long eternity. The phrase which the apostle uses in reference to himself and others of the elect, as descriptive of their state previous to their conversion, can scarcely be mistaken,—"The childen of wrath, even as others." And we appeal to any man, whether this expression does not bear us out in the assertion, that between the elect and the reprobate there really existed no difference whatever, up to the moment when the former believed the gospel, and entered by faith into the full possession of all the privileges of the children of God. It seems plain, then, that viewing men as unbelievers, they all stand upon a common level,—they all occupy the same position,—the position of rebels against God, children of wrath, and heirs of hell.

But the doctrine which we are examining does make

a difference among sinners of the human family, not only before their conversion, but previous to their existence in the world. That doctrine informs us, that "all men are not created to like estate." Some come into the world the elect children of God, chosen into his family and enrolled among the number of his children, ages before they came into being. All the rest come into existence "the children of wrath." Now if this be really true in reference to the former, the question may be boldly proposed in reference to them at any stage of their spiritual history, and during the entire course of their unbelief and rebellion—"Who shall lay anything to their charge?" The simple question is this—Are they not among the number of God's elect? Are they not among the number of those for whom alone (it is affirmed) the Saviour shed his blood? On this single ground, may the unconverted sinner boldly and presumptuously take his stand, and fancy himself safe enough in his sins. Here he may, and here, alas! too many actually do lay themselves quietly down to rest, saying peace, peace, unto their souls, while God is saying, there is no peace; and here, in point of fact, are vast multitudes of men and women making shipwreck of their souls, and rushing heedlessly into an undone eternity.

And here the question meets us: Is not such conduct as this the result of a most palpable abuse of the doctrine now under examination? If such a conclusion as that now indicated, were indeed the effect of the abuse and perversion of the doctrine of the Calvinist, this simple fact would be enough to turn aside the entire edge of the argument we are now pursuing. But this is far from being the case. We have been stating the natural and necessary result, not of the abuse of this doctrine, but of its use. It needs only to be received into the understanding of any man, and believed in as a truth, and consistently followed out, and reduced to practice, in order to leave its votaries at ease in the midst of their unbelief and their sin. Let any man believe it, and what is his argument? He either is, or he is not, one of the elect. If he is, he is safe; for who can lay anything to the charge of God's elect? If, on the other hand, he is not one of the elect, he must needs be among the number of the reprobate, and on this supposition it is vain for him to perplex himself, for who can venture to reverse or to alter the course of God's unalterable decree? Will any man undertake to find a single flaw in reasoning such as this? It is such reasoning as presents itself to every mind, on the simple announcement of the doctrine now under examination. It amounts to nothing less than a very plain and very simple demonstration. It is a conclusion arising most naturally from the doctrine of which we speak, so that any child can draw it for himself. And so be it, that a man can be induced to believe that "all men are not created to like estate," but come into existence either the heirs of heaven on the one hand, or destined to endless misery on the other, we do not see that it is possible for the man, consistently with his belief, to give himself any concern whatever about his soul's salvation. That is a matter settled and arranged, one way or another, long before he came into existence, and why should he presume to usurp the place of God by intermeddling with his most wise and irreversible decree?

It is only when you turn your attention to the text which we have selected from the epistle to the Ephesians, that you will be able to discover wherein the palpable fallacy of all such reasoning really consists. The fallacy is detected in the premises, and not in the conclusion which is deduced therefrom. The foundation is unstable. It is a sandy foundation; and hence the erection which is fairly enough built upon it, totters and falls before the slightest examination. What are the premises from which the false conclusion is legitimately drawn—the foundation on which the tottering fabric is fairly enough built? This is to be seen in the assertion of John Calvin, that "all men are not created to like estate." Here lies the fundamental error,—the error which the Spirit of God emphatically contradicts, when he informs us that even the elect, before they believe the gospel, are ranged among the children of wrath, even as others. So, then, it is most evident that they are not the elect children of God before they believe. They are the children of wrath, and that is, in other words, asserting that they are not the children of God. They cannot be called the children of God and the children of the devil at one and the same moment of time. They cannot, at one and the same moment, have it truly affirmed concerning them, that they "are condemned already, because they believe not," and yet that "none can lay anything to their charge," because they are God's elected and justified children. The plain and unvarnished truth must come out, and stand forth in broad and palpable opposition to the assertion of Calvin,—the assertion which forms the corner-stone of the entire system which goes by his name. It must be admitted that all men are born to like estate. They are every one of them by nature the children of wrath. Jew and Gentile alike, are every soul of them concluded under sin and unbelief, and consequent condemnation. In their natural condition, and in their state of unbelief, there is not one elect child of God among them all. In this state, there is no justification to any one soul among them. There is laid, and laid justly, to their charge, the most tremendous crime that can possibly be laid to the charge of any creature. They are not only standing out rebels against God, but they are making God a liar, so long as they believe not the record which God hath given of his Son. (1st John v. 10, 11.)

Such is the estate—the condition, in which all men are, without exception, placed, before they are actually converted to God. Considering them, then, in this condition, what is the estate to which they are every moment exposed? They are the children of wrath, and in this state they are every hour exposed to the wrath of God and the pains of hell for ever. There is but a step between them and death. The brittle thread of life, and that alone, suspends every soul of them over the pit of endless perdition. In this position it is worse than idle—it is false, utterly false, to say that any single sinner differs from any other sinner of the human race, by being embraced in an absolute or unconditional decree, which insures one unbeliever of heaven, while it destines another unbeliever to hell as his sure and irreversible destiny. Let the words of the Son of God be yet once more sounded in the ears of every unbelieving sinner—"HE THAT BELIEVETH NOT IS CONDEMNED ALREADY." And before these words let the theory perish for ever, which would lead any man to suppose, that there are some UNBELIEVERS against whom no charge can be justly laid, because they happen to be included among God's elect.

II.—WE OBJECT TO THAT THEORY OF ELECTION NOW UNDER EXAMINATION, BECAUSE, IN THE SECOND PLACE, IT FLATLY CONTRADICTS THE SCRIPTURE DECLARATION THAT THERE IS IN THE GOSPEL A MESSAGE OF SALVATION TO EVERY CREATURE.

It will surely be admitted that the message of the gospel is addressed to all men on the face of the earth. There is no distinction—no exception here: "Go ye into all the world, and preach the gospel to every creature." "Behold, I bring you good tidings of great joy, which shall be to all people." These, and such like statements, with which the Word of God abounds, are sufficiently plain and intelligible even to the simplest understanding. By them, the banner of peace is held out to all men. In them, the Holy Spirit is heard addressing the word of salvation to all. And what are these, in point of fact, but the precise tidings referred to so distinctly and so eloquently in the apocalyptic vision, where was seen "another angel flying in the midst of heaven, having the everlasting gospel to preach unto them that dwell on the earth, and to every nation, and kindred, and tongue, and people"? And now, my brethren, will you permit me here to pause in order to ask you one single question, which you are by this time quite prepared to appreciate—What are the good tidings of great joy which the ministers of the gospel have to preach to the reprobate, if the system of Calvinism be true? This is the simple question, which I beg most earnestly to press upon your attention. Does the system now under examination admit of any good tidings whatever to those of the human family whom, it is said, God has determined beforehand eternally to condemn? It is either true, or it is not true, that all men are not created to the like estate, but that to some eternal life, and to others eternal death, is foreappointed by the immutable fiat of the Almighty. If this be true, then let the truth be told, and let it be honestly announced to men, that there is no gospel—no good tidings of great joy—to be preached to any, save only to the elect. If this be true, what is the real state of matters in reference to the great proportion of mankind who do not happen to be elected? God has been pleased to pass them by, and to include them in his reprobating decree, and to bring them into existence for purposes and ends very different (to use the words of Dr. Candlish) from those for which he has created others, inasmuch as he has sold them to his son, in order that his Son may get possession of them, soul and body, for eternal damnation. I wonder not, my friends, that a thrill of horror should pass through your spirits at the bare and simple repetition of that which we are called upon to receive as the truth of God. It is said to be truth; and the question is, whether it be good tidings of great joy. Does it not, on the contrary, exclude the possibility of any good news from God to those who are not elected? It is not like the law, which, though it be not the gospel, is useful as a schoolmaster to lead sinners to Christ, by showing them their need of a Saviour. It is a schoolmaster this, which drives men away from Christ, assuring them, as it does, that there is no atonement for them in his death, but that he has bought them for no other purpose or end, than to exercise his power in tormenting them throughout eternity, unless they are among the number of the elect. But you tell me, that this is not the way in which Calvinistic preachers speak unto sinners; they preach freely and fully, and they assure all men that, whether they be elected or not, they are among those to whom the gospel comes, and to whom its overtures are most earnestly and sincerely made. But what is the sum and substance of all such preaching? What is this but a weekly condemnation of the doctrine which we are now examining—a weekly exposure of it as a forgery and a lie?

It is not possible for any man to announce, in a single sentence, a more palpable contradiction than what is embodied in the twofold announcement—that there is an offer of salvation honestly made to all the reprobated sons of men, and that God sincerely wills them to be saved, while it is at the same time true that God has created them for the single purpose of damnation, so that they must reverse the purpose, and annihilate the decree of God, before they can be saved. I fearlessly put to you all, whether there be not in such a statement a flat and palpable contradiction. What would you say to the man who should style himself a father, and protest over the dead body of his murdered child, that he desired not and willed not that it should die—and who should, at the same instant, point you to the cup of sweetened poison which he had put in its way, so that the little one might be exposed to a temptation which its corruption was not likely to resist, and which the unnatural wretch knew his child would infallibly partake of, and drinking of which it sickened and died? And what will you say of the system which teaches you and your children to believe, that the God of heaven has made a decree from eternity to destroy many of you, and, in order to carry out his purpose, keeps back and withholds what he knows would save you, and farther, exposes you to such objects as he knows will ruin you, and finally gives you over to the power of the devil?—what do you think of the system which insists upon you swallowing all this as truth, and at the same time turns round upon you with a smile and assures you, that there is a sincere offer of salvation to you in the gospel, and that God does sincerely desire you to be saved? Are we uncharitable when we say, that all this is a mere mockery of human wretchedness? Is it wonderful that the men who tell you all this, should at the same time assure you, that you cannot believe it? The wonder would be if men could believe an announcement which is self-contradictory and absurd; and the most marvellous thing of all is, that men of common sense should not only tolerate, but applaud and support and encourage, by their influence and example, so glaring and so monstrous a mockery of all that is sacred and precious to souls passing onwards to the judgment-seat of God.

But we are told, in reply to all this, that, in the first place, men have nothing to do with election in preaching the gospel to sinners; and, in the second place, that those to whom the gospel comes are not supposed to know whether they are among the elect or among the reprobate. I crave your attention, very briefly, to this specious reply. It is said that they to whom the gospel is preached have nothing to do with the doctrine now under examination. I ask, Why then insist upon men receiving it? If sinners have nothing to do with it, why place it in the forefront of your creed, and compel your very children to imbibe it as with their mother's milk? But if it be true, it is not right to say that men have nothing to do with it; for if it be true, it manifests to all men the startling fact, that there is no gospel at all to any save the elect; and if there be no gospel to any save the elect, then there should be no preaching to any except the elect, and it would ultimately come to this, that there would be no congregations and no preachers at all. In this way, "this our craft is in danger to be set at nought," and hence it is necessary and expedient to say to men, that the doctrine of election is a mystery with which they have nothing whatever to do!

And it does not make matters any better to affirm, in the second place, that men cannot say whether they are among the elect or among the reprobate. This state of ignorance does not alter the fact, that, according to this doctrine, there are no good news whatever to those who are not elected. The fact still stands out, that there is no gospel to preach to the reprobate. But while the ignorance of men does not, and cannot, alter this fact, it renders the preaching of the gospel a dead letter even to the elect. For, with the idea in your minds that there are many, for example, in this present audience, who cannot possibly be saved, because Jesus did not make atonement for you all,—and God, for anything you know, has included many of you in the decree of condemnation, and brought many of you into existence for the express purpose of damnation,—with this idea in your minds, and without any means of ascertaining who the persons are who are thus excluded from the very possibility of salvation, every soul of you must either leave this house careless about the matter, or go away anxiously inquiring—"Is it I? —Is it I?"

In this case, your very ignorance as to whether you are among the elect or the reprobate, must needs prevent even the elect among you from ascertaining and believing that there is really good news this evening announced to you. And hence, alas! it has come to this pass, that under the direful influence of the doctrine we have been examining, it has become a mere matter of course for whole congregations to come and go, week after week and year after year, without any personal appreciation of the great salvation on the one hand, or any anxious inquiry after it on the other. But whenever any season of refreshing does arrive, and the gospel is preached and received with power from on high, sinners are called upon to cast away from their minds the ideas of election which we have been looking at—to treat them as if they had no existence—and simply to believe, each man for himself and each woman for herself, the message of the gospel, as addressed personally to each. All this is a good confession of the truth of what we now assert, when we ask you to reject the doctrine of Calvin and the Confession for this reason, that it most glaringly contradicts the Bible, wherein we are assured that there is a gospel—a true gospel—glad tidings, indeed, to every soul of man, which we are privileged and commanded to preach unto you.

What then shall we say to you, in conclusion, but call upon you to receive, without one moment's delay, what the Holy Ghost, speaking through his servant Jude, graciously styles "THE COMMON SALVATION."

There is no restriction expressed in the Word of God, and most assuredly there is no restriction implied. The God with whom we have to do is not, like the dark genius of Calvinism, a deceitful and a deceiving spirit. He is a God of truth, and without iniquity; just and right is he. He is not only the just God, but also the Saviour; and in this precise character has he revealed himself unto the guilty sons of men. "Look unto me, and be ye saved, all the ends of the earth, for I am God, and besides me there is none else." (Isaiah xlv. 21, 22.) There is assuredly a gospel for you all, and this is only another mode of assuring you, that no frowning decree intercepts between any of you and salvation.

The glorious gospel which we announce to you, does not indeed say to you that you are pardoned and saved, but it comes with such a message as this to no single individual on the face of the earth. It does not tell any man that he is already pardoned and saved. It proceeds upon an assumption the very reverse of all this. It assumes truly that the sinners to whom it comes, are already condemned and ruined; and assuredly there is nothing indicated thereby, which is either fitted or intended to leave any soul among you all, even for a single moment, at peace in your sins; but you are thereby assured, that now your sins form no reason why any sinner among you should, even for a single moment, remain without peace with your God. "Behold the Lamb of God." "Behold the Lamb of God bearing away the sin of the world." (John i.

29, 36.) "He is the propitiation for our sins, and not for ours only, but also for the sins of the whole world." (1 John ii. 2.) This is the gospel message to every creature, and it forms the sum and substance of the gospel message to you.

That such is the gospel message, addressed by the Holy Spirit to condemned and ruined sinners, and to every sinner condemned and ruined on the face of the earth, is abundantly manifest from the Word of God. Take one single example from among the multitude of instances which the Bible contains. It is written in 1 Cor. xv. 1–4: "Moreover, brethren, I declare unto you THE GOSPEL which I preached unto you, which also ye have received, and wherein ye stand; by which also ye are saved, if ye keep in memory what I preached unto you, unless ye have believed in vain: for I delivered unto you first of all that which I also received, how that CHRIST DIED FOR OUR SINS according to the Scriptures; and that HE WAS BURIED, AND THAT HE ROSE AGAIN the third day according to the Scriptures." Here, then, we have the testimony of Inspiration upon this most momentous of all questions. Here we are informed, by the inspired apostle himself, what he preached to the heathen Corinthians—"first of all," before they believed—when first he made his appearance among them as an ambassador of Christ. It was not that Christ died for the sins of the elect, or for the sins of believers only. This would have been sad news indeed to those poor heathens who were at the time unsaved—who were at the time unbelievers—and who must have concluded infallibly, from such a message, that seeing they were unbelievers, Christ did not shed his blood for them. If Jesus died for believers only, and if this was the gospel which Paul preached unto a company of heathen unbelievers, when first of all he went among them, you will see at once, that such a gospel as this was anything but good news TO THEM. It was tantamount to a message of exclusion to every unbeliever in whose hearing it was announced—exclusion from the very possibility of salvation; for if Jesus did not die for their sins, how could any soul among them possibly be saved? They were unbelievers—and to say to them first of all, that Christ died for believers, was just to announce the very reverse of gospel—it was just to assure them that for their sins no atonement had been made, and consequently that for them there existed no possibility of escape from the wrath to come. To tell a company of unbelievers that Christ died for believers, is assuredly the most effectual of all possible devices whereby the poor souls may be shut up in their unbelief—shut out from the very possibility of believing. It is just another mode of saying to them—"Christ DID NOT die for you." But this is "ANOTHER GOSPEL." This is not the gospel which Paul declares he was privileged and commanded to preach. His first message to those heathen men and heathen women was—"Christ died for our sins, and was buried, and rose again the third day, according to the Scriptures." This was the gospel which he preached. This was the gospel which they received after it was first of all preached unto them, and by the faith of which they were saved. "Christ died for our sins," said the inspired preacher, and by this saying he assured every one of those to whom he spoke, that the blood of the Son of God was shed for their sins as well as for the sins of the man who addressed them. There was SOMETHING here for every one of them to believe, and that something was—"the gospel"—"good tidings of great joy" to every sinner among them. Christ died for you and also for me. "The Son of God loved me, and gave himself for me;" but his love encircled you as well as me, and he died for your sins as well as for mine. He died for the sins of every one of us. "He died FOR OUR SINS, according to the Scriptures," and his death has been accepted and acknowledged by God as a complete satisfaction for all our guilt. In testimony of this, God has raised him from the grave, for "he was buried, and rose again the third day according to the Scriptures." Do you not behold here, my fellow-sinners, something very different from that undefined and indefinable system of mysticism and delusion under which the souls of our countrymen have been bound down and shackled, and before which, thousands and tens of thousands are daily and hourly perishing? Do you not apprehend, in this inspired narrative of what the gospel message is, something very plain and very simple and very cheering for you and me to believe? It is not that Jesus, when he died, did everything for the elect and nothing at all for the reprobate—everything for believers and nothing at all for unbelievers—everything for some favoured individuals and perhaps nothing for you. That is not what you are called upon to believe, for all that is a delusion and a lie. Neither is it, that there is in the death of Christ a "special and exclusive reference" to the elect, and a more "general reference" to the world. This is only another and more specious aspect of the same delusion, whereby the credit of a tottering system of theology is sought to be upheld at the expense of the souls of men. This is that delusion whereby men are instructed to admit, that Jesus died for all, and therefore for each, while a bare PERADVENTURE is left behind and beneath this gospel-like admission, and whereby no man is informed whether the Son of God, by his death upon the cross, made a true and proper satisfaction for his sins. In the face of this device, whereby every sinner is taught that, *in a certain sense,* Jesus died for all, and therefore for him, the man is still left to doubt and hesitate and conjecture and inquire whether he be among the number of those who are "*specially interested*" in the death of the Son of God. You are not, therefore, called upon by God to believe that Jesus did something for the world and another thing for the elect when he shed his blood upon the cross. This general and special-reference device is really a far more dangerous, because a far more subtle delusion, than is the barefaced falsehood against which we have already guarded you. The truth of the gospel is, that Jesus died EQUALLY for all men. He satisfied God for the sins of every man as truly and properly as for the sins of any man. His love was equal love to all. His death was a complete and perfect satisfaction to the law and justice of God for the sins of all men, without distinction and without exception. Rejoice, O sinner, in the gladsome intelligence, that NOTHING WHATEVER EXCLUSIVE OF YOU was done upon the cross when the Saviour of the world exclaimed, "IT IS FINISHED, and bowed his head and gave up the ghost!" The non-elect as well as the elect—unbelievers as well as believers—have an equal interest in the great propitiation. Does this announcement startle you?—does it dispose you to inquire, "Has Jesus shed his blood in vain"?—or, does it incline you to rush on to the conclusion that, on this supposition, all men must needs be pardoned and justified and redeemed and saved? Be pleased, then, to mark well the error which lies at the foundation of this very prevalent misconception. The error lies in confounding the atonement of the Son of God with its saving and sanctifying results. The atonement is one thing—the result of the atonement is another and a different thing altogether. When the Saviour shed his blood upon the cross, the work of atonement was finished—ample satisfaction was there and then made for the sins of every sinner in whose room and stead the Saviour died—but it is a mistake to imagine that there and then every sinner for whom the Saviour died was actually pardoned and justified and redeemed and sanctified and saved. The death of the Son of God ought not thus to be confounded with its multiform and glorious results. This death was the propitiation or atonement for sin. But the atonement is not pardon nor justification nor redemption nor sanctification nor complete and ultimate salvation. The atonement, or the death of Christ, forms THE GROUND of pardon and justification and redemption, and all the kindred blessings enjoyed by believers; but every man can easily distinguish between the ground upon which any blessing is bestowed and the blessing itself, even as it is no difficult task for any one of you to see the distinction between the foundation and the building which is thereon erected. No man doubts that Jesus, by his death, made atonement, for example, for the sins of Saul of Tarsus, but few men will affirm, in so many words, that Saul of Tarsus was justified and sanctified and saved when the Saviour died.* But all that Jesus did and suffered—all that Jesus by his death actually accomplished for Saul of Tarsus, was completely finished upon the cross. The matter of fact is therefore easily enough ascertained. The man of whom we speak was neither justified nor sanctified till, on his road to Damascus, he was graciously brought to believe in Him whom he had, up till that moment, so madly persecuted. This simple statement involves no difficult or thorny controversy. It is a statement of a fact, which the plainest mind can easily substantiate. The man was condemned

* It is remarkable that even Dr. A. MARSHALL, of Kirkintilloch, should affirm the death of Christ to be, in itself, "THE REDEMPTION of his people." But here lies the fundamental error of the Calvinistic system.

UNTIL he believed. But Jesus died for his sins BEFORE he believed. The atonement was finished for him; but still, in the face of that atonement, he was for many a long year and day under condemnation,—a child of wrath, even as others. Although his sins were atoned for by the death of Christ, Saul of Tarsus remained unjustified, unsanctified, unsaved. It is surely evident, from this simple fact, that there is a mighty difference between the atonement and justification, or sanctification, or redemption. But if the death of Christ had indeed been the justification of his people—or if it had been the sanctification of his people—or, yet once more, if this death had in itself been the redemption of his people—it would have followed from all this, that Saul of Tarsus would have been justified and sanctified and redeemed from the moment that Jesus expired upon the cross. He would have been justified and sanctified and redeemed at the very time when he himself informs us that he was a child of wrath and an heir of hell. And so there would have been no need of the Holy Spirit to lead him to believe, and there would be no need of faith as the instrumental cause of justification or sanctification or redemption in the case of any sinner for whom the Saviour died. It is most evident, from such considerations as these, that Christ did not intend, by the act of dying alone, to justify or sanctify or redeem one single sinner for whom he died. But he did all that he intended to do. He did not die in vain. He finished the work given him to do. He made an atonement for sin, and thereby he opened up the way through which any, and every sinner, might be pardoned, justified, sanctified, redeemed, and glorified through the faith of the truth. It is for this reason that every blessing is traced to the death of Jesus, as when it is said, for example, in Rom. v. 9, that we are "JUSTIFIED BY HIS BLOOD." This statement does not contradict the statement in the first verse of the same chapter, wherein we are said to be "JUSTIFIED BY FAITH," and we are not to infer therefrom that the shedding of the blood of Jesus was the actual justification of his people, or that any man among them is actually justified before he believes the gospel. And so for the same reason Christ is said by his death to have redeemed us from the curse of the law, not as if any man is actually redeemed from the curse any more than he is actually justified while he remains in unbelief, but that the ground, the all-sufficient ground, the only meritorious and God-glorifying and law-magnifying ground of our redemption has been laid in the obedience unto the death of the Son of God. What then does the Holy Spirit do when he would impart saving faith to you, by holding up before you the death of Jesus as the propitiation for your sins? Does he ask you to believe that you are pardoned already, or that you are already justified? His testimony to you implies the very reverse. You stand out condemned and lost—on the very brink of eternal destruction. This is the faithful testimony of Him who earnestly desires you to flee from the wrath to come. But this is only one-half of his testimony. He tells you that the great atoning sacrifice, on the ground of which you may, this very hour, be pardoned and justified and saved, was eighteen hundred years ago offered up for your sins, and not only offered up, but accepted by God himself as a complete answer for every one of your transgressions. He points you to God, not relentless but propitiated, and ready freely to justify you for the sake of what his dear Son did and suffered in your room and stead. Think, then, my unconverted hearers, of the awful position which YOU DO OCCUPY. You are on the brink of hell every moment you remain without a personal appreciation of the Saviour as all your own. Think again of the position YOU MAY occupy, even in the twinkling of an eye. There is not one hair's-breadth between any of you and salvation. The Son of God has shed his blood for your every sin, and it needs but THE TURNING OF YOUR MIND —the turning of your mind, which, like the lightning's rapid glance, can speed in an instant from hell to heaven,—to flee from impending wrath, and hide your guilty souls under the covert of your Saviour's righteousness. "Repent ye, therefore, and be converted, that your sins may be blotted out, when the times of refreshing shall come from the presence of the Lord." How long will any of you remain careless and at your ease, as if the thunderbolt of impending wrath were not hanging over your faithless and Saviour-despising souls! How long will others of you labour in vain, to justify yourselves in the sight of your God by your unbelieving efforts, as if an ample ground for your immediate pardon and justification had not been already furnished by the death of Jesus! To remain in your present state of mind is to lull yourselves to repose on the brink of a tremendous precipice, over which, if once you fall, you shall rise no more for ever. To summon up your most serious and devoted efforts to extricate your souls from the position which you occupy, is but to insure your destruction. Your safety lies not in remaining where you are, and far less does it lie in summoning up your energies to move. You are stretched upon the very brink of destruction, and the arm of Another alone can save you. Already, O sinner, is that arm outstretched. It is the right arm of Him who is "MIGHTY TO SAVE." Why, then, should you hesitate to trust implicitly in your Saviour's love, or question for a moment the perfection or the efficacy of his finished atonement? Why should you, on the one hand, endeavour to lull your souls into a fatal repose, by greedily imbibing a false and delusive opiate; or vainly struggle, on the other hand, to move from your present perilous position, by summoning yourselves to some effort of your own? Why not at once awake, and open your eyes to a full perception of the awful position in which you are actually remaining, and, at the same time, behold the gracious Saviour who has stretched out his arm to save you, and forthwith intrust your souls implicitly to his hand? I have spoken to you of an opiate, the tendency whereof is only to lull your spirits into a dangerous repose. That opiate is neither more nor less than the fatal error which I have been endeavouring to expose. Let any man imagine that when the Saviour died, he actually pardoned, justified, or redeemed all for whom he shed his blood, and his every effort will be to get himself to believe that he is already pardoned, justified, and redeemed, unless, indeed, he can succeed in banishing the subject entirely from his mind. I have also spoken to you of an effort to move the soul from the perilous position in which every unbeliever is placed—an effort which, if successful, is successful only for destruction. That effort is also the result of fundamental error on the nature of the atonement. Let any man imagine that, though Jesus died for his sins, he nevertheless left the man something or other himself to do, before he can consistently be pardoned or justified or saved, and he will assuredly be induced to pray in unbelief, or to labour in unbelief, or to wait on in unbelief, most earnestly desiring to perceive some tokens for THE BETTER within his soul or about his life, before he will venture to trust for eternity in the glorious efficacy of the great propitiation. On either supposition the soul is lost—lost for ever, solely as the result of culpably misunderstanding the gospel and "neglecting the great salvation." There exists but one only safeguard against such prevalent, and all but universal delusion. That safeguard is to be discovered in the Word of God alone, as opposed to the erroneous systems of fallible men. In that only infallible record, every soul of man is faithfully warned of the awful position in which he is positively placed up to the moment of conversion. And in that blessed Bible every sinner of the human race is earnestly and compassionately directed at once to the converting truth. This is all expressed in the simple announcement, "Christ died for our sins, and was buried, and rose again the third day." The moment any sinner apprehends the true meaning of this one truthful and glorious announcement, in its gracious bearing towards his guilty and condemned and ruined soul, that moment is he saved. Yet once more then do we urge, and entreat, and implore you to "Behold the Lamb of God." He has taken away the sin of the world, and assuredly, my dear friends, your sins have not been left behind, as an insuperable barrier to your immediate escape. They are every one of them away—for ever away. They formed part and parcel of that tremendous burden, which pressed down the Lord of Glory to the dust of death. For all our sins, and for the sins of all amongst us, did the Saviour die, according to the Scriptures. But he is no longer in the grave: "He is risen as he said." He rose again on the morning of the third day, according to the Scriptures; but when he rose again, O sinner, thy sins did not rise along with him, to scare thee, even for an instant, from the bosom of thy God. O no! Blessed—for ever blessed be his gracious and glorious name, that bosom of infinite compassion, even while I speak, upheaves with tender emotion, and swells well-nigh to bursting, in the full view of thy wretchedness and thy danger. The heart of thy God is filled with earnest and sincere longings after thy immediate salvation. Can it be, O sinner, that in the full view of all this, you yourself have no pity upon your own immortal soul? Or can it be that, in the view of all this, you will still hesitate, and doubt, and suspect your Saviour's love, as if he were frowning you away from him even now, and commanding you with a stern voice to make yourself somewhat more comely, before he can receive you? You would "wait till you are better!" You would be somewhat more righteous, at least in thine own eyes, and then you will venture to assure yourself of acceptance. And thus it is, O vain man, that thou answerest thy Saviour's tender entreaty; and thus it is that thou dost venture to give the lie to his gracious declaration, wherein he says, "I came not to call the RIGHTEOUS, but SINNERS, to repentance." But thus it is, that you are up to this very hour afraid to meet thy God, because, in point of fact, thy sinful, unbelieving, doubting soul is unprepared to face him at the bar of judgment. Well mayest thou tremble at the thought of death, judgment, and eternity, seeing that thou wilt not tremble at the thought of casting behind thee this thy day of gracious, merciful visitation; trampling under foot thy Saviour's blood; wasting thy hour of grace in thoughtless carelessness, or laborious self-righteousness, or damning doubts. Would to God, O sinner, that those salutary fears of thine would rise into a hurricane of anxiety and alarm, and, ere it be too late, shiver into atoms that false refuge under which you actually manage to lull your soul to temporary repose. Would to God that you were driven from every lying refuge, under which thousands of sober, serious professors are saying, "Peace, peace," and were led to betake thyself at once to the only refuge which can shield thee from the coming storm, the only covert which can shelter thee from the approaching tempest. Abandon, then, we earnestly beseech you, the false and unscriptural theology—the thing which men call gospel—all of which any man may believe, and yet have no solid peace in the prospect of meeting God,—all of which a man may believe, and yet doubt his soul's salvation,—all of which a man may believe, and yet remain unsaved. Bring this soul-destroying delusion to the touchstone of the Bible. Compare it with the glorious gospel which Paul preached, and behold the contrast!

"O! how unlike the complex works of man,
Heaven's easy, artless, unencumber'd plan;
No meretricious graces to beguile,
No clustering ornaments to clog the pile;
From ostentation as from weakness free,
It stands, like the cerulean arch we see,
Majestic in its own simplicity.
Inscribed above the portal from afar,
Conspicuous as the brightness of a star,
Legible only by the light they give,
Stand the soul-quickening words—BELIEVE AND LIVE."

LECTURE SECOND.

THE CALVINIAN DOCTRINE OPPOSED TO REASON—SUBVERSIVE OF FREE GRACE IN THE JUSTIFICATION OF THE BELIEVER —QUOTATION FROM DR. PAYNE AND ANDREW FULLER —CALVINISM ALLIED TO SOCINIANISM—CONCLUDING REMARKS.

EPHES. ii. 5:—"By grace ye are saved."

BEFORE resuming our consideration of the doctrine of election, as that doctrine is exhibited in Calvinistic creeds, we would here solicit your attention to a very plain and a very important distinction. We refer to the distinction which obtains between what is above reason, and what is contrary to reason. There is very much connected with almost every subject of human investigation, which is admittedly beyond the reach of human reason. There are heights which the human imagination in its loftiest soarings cannot reach; there are depths which the soundings of the human intellect cannot fathom; there is a length and a breadth across which the mind of man has never dared to travel—a boundless region, in the immensity which stretches out before the research of the human soul, which it is impossible for man in the present stage of his existence to examine and explore. It is plain, therefore, that "here we see through a glass darkly," and "know only in part," so that there are many things we cannot fully understand, which it is our duty nevertheless to believe on the simple authority of God. We may specify, by way of example, the doctrine of the trinity in unity—three persons and yet one God—a plain and manifest truth revealed by God for the belief of man. This is an example of a doctrine which is above reason, but which, when properly explained as it is announced in the Scriptures, is in no way contrary to reason. It involves no contradiction. It lands us in no glaring or palpable absurdity. The reception of it as a truth, forces us to contradict and explain away not one solitary declaration contained within the ample range of the revealed word. Thus it is with many doctrines which we receive without any hesitation. For reason herself chimes in here with the voice of revelation, and it is fully consistent with the dictates of the soundest philosophy, to receive with the docility of a little child whatever is contained in the Word of God, even though the doctrine should be to us enshrouded in a cloud of mystery. The clearly ascertained and well accredited statements of the Word of God are to be received without any debate, as so many facts; And the soundest philosophy and the strongest common sense demand, in behalf of a clearly ascertained fact, the profoundest homage of the soul. A well accredited fact instantly takes the place of an axiom, to dispute which, or to argue inconsistently with which, is to be guilty of a most flagrant sin against the highest reason, and to subvert the foundations of truth. It matters not whether a man can account for it or not,—if it be a thing which is ascertained to be a fact, it must be received. It matters not whether we can explain it or not—there it is, standing out before our eyes an undisputed fact, and by that every theory must be tested, and stand or fall as it agrees with, or differs from, what is thus ascertained to be verily true.

We ought therefore every one of us to understand, that if the theory now under examination were merely above reason, this would not form of itself any just ground for its rejection. If it were a doctrine admittedly and indisputably revealed in the Word of God, that simple circumstance would be itself sufficient to demand and to secure its immediate reception by every man amongst us, however strange or mysterious the doctrine might appear. In this case all that could be said of it would be, that it is above reason, but that would really be saying nothing whatever which would prejudice a single reasonable man against its reception as a doctrine from God, and according to godliness.

The case would be entirely altered if it could be affirmed of any doctrine, that it is contrary to reason. Such, for example, is the Popish doctrine of transubstantiation. It is contrary to reason to dispute the evidence of our senses, and when the Papist informs us that the bread and the wine at the Supper of the Lord are not bread and wine, but form part and parcel of the real body and blood of Christ, it would be absurd to believe it, because our senses inform us of the very reverse. Now, it is no less contrary to reason to admit any theory to be true, which plainly contradicts some of the most obvious truths which the Word of God contains. As we have already noticed, whatever is plainly revealed in the Bible must be received as truth; and should any doctrine be brought before us which is manifestly inconsistent with anything which is thus plainly revealed, that doctrine would thereby stand out detected and exposed as an imposition and a falsehood.

It will be readily admitted by you all, that the Bible is not, and cannot be, in one single item really and truly inconsistent with itself. To suppose the reverse of this—to suppose that in any one point there exists any contradiction or inconsistency in the Scriptures, amounts to nothing less than a rejection of them, as the infallible record of the infallible God. But you will remember that, in the outset of this investigation, we stated it distinctly as one of those principles which we take to be admitted on all hands, that the Bible is indeed the book of God. We are not now engaged in a discussion with men who deny this fundamental point. And admitting, as we presume you all do, that this blessed volume is indeed a message from God to man, we now solemnly and affectionately call upon you to act reasonably and consistently with this admission, and to reject, without any hesitation, whatever doctrine is seen by you to be evidently opposed to some of the most obvious statements of divine revelation.

You will require to keep steadily before your minds what the doctrine is, which we are engaged in examining. As that doctrine is briefly stated by its founder, John Calvin, himself, it asserts that "all men are not created to like estate"—some of the human race, according to this brief and emphatic statement, coming into existence elect infants, unconditionally and irreversibly destined to eternal happiness; all the rest of mankind coming into existence, unconditionally doomed to everlasting damnation. The former class are accordingly represented as being exclusively interested in the death of the Son of God, viewing that sacrifice as a propitiation or atonement for sin. All the rest of mankind, excepting the elect, having no interest whatever in the atonement or death of Christ, are said by this theology to belong to Christ for no other end or purpose than that he may exercise his power in consigning them to damnation. You will remember that we have been careful not to misstate or to exaggerate the doctrine which we have engaged to examine, and therefore we have quoted at some length the very words of the most respectable and distinguished of its supporters, not forgetting to set before you the words of the Confession of Faith, wherein it is found. The words of the most eminent man, perhaps, among the modern advocates of the doctrine, are no less clear and decisive than those of Calvin himself; Dr. Candlish having very lately published the statement, that the reprobate belong to Christ to be judged or condemned, while the elect are his to be saved. The language of this modern Calvinist is, as we have seen at length in the former lecture, very emphatic upon the point. He speaks of the death of Christ, and he declares it to be no atonement, no ransom properly so called for the great majority of mankind, viz., the reprobate. The words of Dr. Candlish, as you will remember, are the following, in reference to all men, women, and children excepting the elect:—"He [Christ] has won them—bought them, if you will—but it is that he may so dispose of them as to glorify the retributive righteousness of God in their condemnation."

So far then as our argument has been laid before you for consideration, we have endeavoured to prove that this doctrine is diametrically opposed to two of the plainest principles of God's most holy Word.

It is perfectly plain, from the whole tenor of the Word of God, that no man is safe for one moment while he remains in unbelief. This we affirm to be one of the most obvious of all the principles or truths exhibited in the Bible. And inasmuch as the doctrine of election exhibited by Calvin, Candlish, and the Confession seems to be directly opposed to this plainly revealed principle of God's Word, we have spoken of it as not only false, but ruinous and destructive to the souls of men.

It is still farther evident from the Word of God, that the gospel contains good tidings of great joy to every creature, so that there does not now exist, and there never did exist, and there never can exist, one single sinner on the face of the earth to whom a message of salvation is not therein exhibited. But the doctrine of Calvin directly contradicts this plain and obvious fact, and is once more proved to be unscriptural and false.

III. THE THIRD OBJECTION WHICH I NOW STATE TO THIS DOCTRINE IS, THAT IT IS SUBVERSIVE OF THE BIBLE PRINCIPLE OF SALVATION BY FREE GRACE.

If there be one truth more plainly revealed in the Word of God than another, it is the principle of grace—free grace, in the salvation of all who believe. "By grace ye are saved." The assertion of this great truth constituted the sum and substance of apostolic preaching. This was the alpha and the omega, the beginning and the ending of all their sermons. This was the great and glorious announcement around which all their arguments and persuasions revolved, as round a centre of light and love. This was the burden of all their inspired epistles to the various churches over which they sedulously and carefully watched, even as they who were to give an account. "By grace ye are saved, through faith; and that not of yourselves; it is the gift of God; not of works, lest any man should boast." This was the truth in which they gloried, and for any man to subvert, or even to depreciate the great doctrine of salvation by free grace, was to aim a deadly thrust at the very heart of the glorious gospel of the grace of God.

And as it was in ancient times, so it is now, and so it will ever be. The grand characteristic of the Bible is, that it is a revelation of grace. This is the most striking feature of the blessed gospel; and it is mainly because the doctrine which we are now examining, is a direct and impious subversion of the grace of God in the salvation of the sinner, that it eats out the very vitals of the gospel in our beloved land.

We are anxious in this place not to be misunderstood. We do not say that this theory of the Calvinist is inconsistent with the grace of God in the provision of the atonement. We affirm its utter inconsistency with the manifestation of grace, in the justification and subsequent salvation of the believer. This circumstance has already induced many distinguished Calvinists to make an attempt so far to modify their system of theology, as to make a voluntary surrender of the main position in defence of which the late work of Dr. Candlish was written and published. Some of the most eminent and pious of the Calvinistic clergy have already very candidly admitted the truth and force of the grave accusation we have now made against the system; and, in consistency with this admission, they have very conclusively argued in favour of the great and glorious truth, that Jesus died for all men, and by his death made satisfaction for the sins of the entire human race without one single exception. We shall, in due time, point out to you the inconsistency of this important admission with those Calvinian tenets which such authors still retain. In the meantime, we make the two following quotations from the published works of avowed Calvinists, in order to show you, that the very grave objection now adduced against the theory we are examining, is candidly admitted even by men of most orthodox repute.

The theory of an atonement for the elect alone has been rejected by Dr. Wardlaw, on account of "ITS EXCLUDING EVERY THING OF THE NATURE OF GRACE from every part of the process of the sinner's salvation, excepting the original appointment of the surety, whose payment, in each case, of the estimated debt, cancels the bond, and renders the liberation of the debtor not gracious but obligatory."—*Discourses on the Atonement*, p. 63.

The same objection has been urged against the theory by Dr. George Payne of Exeter, in his Ninth Lecture on Sovereignty, &c. At page 148 of his book, this writer observes:—

"1st, That it renders the deliverance of the elect from punishment a matter of justice to them. They may claim it as a right. It is, in this point of view, as if the atonement were the payment of a pecuniary debt, and is not less incompatible with the notion that grace is exercised in the pardon of sin. There may, indeed, consistently with this opinion, have been grace in the acceptance and in the provision of a substitute; but surely, if that substitute endured the precise amount of punishment which the strong arm of the law would have otherwise laid upon those whom he represented, there can be no grace in remitting it afterwards to them."

In concert with the two distinguished writers from whom we have now quoted, we would raise our testimony against the doctrine of an election of some men only to an exclusive interest in the death of the Son of God; and this we do for the most valid of all reasons,—it is subversive of the grace of God in the justification of believers. What is grace? It is free, unmerited favour; it is unconstrained, voluntary, generous love to those who might justly be condemned. That alone is grace. If it be constrained, it is not grace. If it be merited, it is not grace. If it may not righteously and justly be withheld, it is not grace.

And what is the all but unanimous voice of Calvinistic Scotland? It is that God is bound in justice to save all the elect. Mark it well, my beloved brethren, God is said to be bound in justice to save every soul of man who enters the paradise above. I put it to yourselves if this be not the all but universal shout which proceeds from the hosts of the orthodox when they would act valiantly, and buckle on their armour to do battle against an imaginary heresy. Is not this the universal cry—the watchword of the party:—"Jesus did not, could not, die for all men; for, if he did, then all men would infallibly be saved"? And why? Wherefore is it said to follow, as an obvious conclusion, that all men must be saved if Jesus did (as we say he did) give himself, and shed his precious blood, a ransom for all? The answer is at hand, and it is this: "Because God is bound in justice to save all for whom the Saviour shed his blood, and he would act unjustly if he did not save them."

Where, then, I ask, is the GRACE of God in their

salvation? If God is bound in justice to save those whom he does save, is there a man or woman in this audience who does not see at once the obvious and palpable conclusion? The inevitable conclusion is, that they are indebted not to grace, but to justice, for their salvation. If any one among you is bound in justice to act in a certain way, and if you would be chargeable with injustice were you to refuse so to act, who would think of praising or extolling your generosity when the deed was done? In this case, it is surely evident to you all, that you would be placed under a necessity of acting, so that no thanks to you for granting what you dare not honestly and justly and righteously withhold. Will any man deny that if you were my debtor, and if your debt is paid—if the uttermost farthing has been wrung from you—and if I seek, in the face of this, to lay hold of you, in order to imprison you for the debt, you are in a position to defy me to my face? And what would you think of me, and what would you not say of me, if I were seeking to take credit to myself for most wonderful generosity and grace, simply because I did not throw you into prison? You see at once, from this simple case, that what I am bound in justice to do, so that I would act unjustly if I did not do it, ceases, for that plain and obvious reason, to be an act of grace. The principle is not altered by making the supposition that the debt is paid, not by you but by your cautioner. The simple question between you and me is this: "Is the debt discharged, or is it not?" If it be discharged, then I am bound in justice to set you free from all farther obligation. If the debt be not discharged, and you come to me, saying, "Forgive me my debt," the fact of your asking a free forgiveness of it is, on your part, an acknowledgment that you are dependent upon my grace, and cannot—dare not—appeal to my justice for the discharge. If you say, "Forgive me my debts," and I freely forgive you all, though in justice I be not bound to forgive you aught, then, and then only, may I speak of grace.

Let this very obvious principle be applied to the case in hand. We may very easily perceive, from the principles of the false and unscriptural theology of the day, that the grace of God in saving the sinner is thereby denied and subverted. The system of Calvin, Candlish, and the Confession, speaks plainly out upon this head. It says in plain and express and definite words, that God cannot, without the most glaring injustice, lay a condemning hand upon one soul of the elect. The elect, accordingly, may defy God to condemn them. They are, according to this theory, in a position to march up to the gate of heaven and demand admission. They have no need to say to God, "Father, forgive us our debts;" they have only to remind him that he dare not exact them without acting unjustly, and thereby shaking the pillars of his government and subverting the foundations of his throne. If they were to say, "forgive us our debts," they would thereby recede from the claim of justice, and fall back upon the acknowledgment of grace. But this they cannot do without casting their doctrine of election to the winds; for that doctrine teaches them, that their sins do not need to be forgiven, seeing that these same sins are imagined to be real, literal debts, which were eighteen hundred years ago most fully discharged; and therefore, as an act of common justice, cannot now be brought up against them!

May I not here, my friends, most earnestly and solemnly press upon your attention the simple but very striking fact, that our blessed Saviour has taught all who will take HIM as their teacher, daily and hourly to pray, "Forgive us our debts as we forgive our debtors"? Are you taught by Jesus himself to suppose that sin is a literal debt, so that God is by his death bound in justice to forgive you? Does HE teach you that your heavenly Father would act unjustly by you if he did not pardon your iniquities? No verily. The forgiveness which, for Christ's sake, is free to all—proclaimed in the gospel to all—pressed most earnestly and sincerely upon the acceptance of all—is not an act of justice but an act of grace. And when our Saviour taught and encouraged his disciples daily to pray for it, and daily to appropriate the blessing as their own he sent them, not to a throne of justice, but to the throne of grace. And, in this very prayer, the greatest and best of teachers most emphatically contradicts and condemns the theory, that God would act unjustly if he did not justify every sinner for whom he died.

There is one other consideration, which I beg, in

this connexion, to submit to your attention. If it would be unjust in God to condemn any (for whom Jesus died) in eternity, it would be no less unjust to condemn them in time. If the death of his Son has secured immunity for all for whom he died, in a future world, so that it would be unjust in God to condemn them there, it must have secured the same thing for them in this present world, so that it is no less unjust for him to condemn them here, while they are yet upon the earth. You will notice, what we are called upon to believe, by this doctrine which we are examining. We are called upon to believe, that it would be unjust in God to condemn the elect, simply and exclusively because Jesus bore the condemnation in their room and stead. Now, the simple question to be solved, is a question relating to a matter of fact. Does God not, in point of fact, condemn those for whom the Saviour died? If it would be unjust in God to condemn them because Jesus died for them, we may rest assured that they would never be condemned during any single stage or period of their existence. But it is a fact which cannot be denied, that even the elect are condemned before they believe. It cannot, therefore, be inconsistent with the justice of God to condemn sinners even though Christ has borne the punishment of their sins. If it would be unjust in God to condemn those for whom Christ died, how comes it to pass that in the face of the death of their substitute, they are at any time the children of wrath even as others? It will not be asserted that the mere circumstance of time or place can alter the nature of justice. Neither will it be asserted, that the mere circumstance of a sinner believing or not believing, can make that act of God an act of justice to-day which to-morrow would be most glaringly unjust. Take the case of a debtor and his creditor, as an illustration of this principle to which we now advert. If the creditor is satisfied by having received ample payment, it would be unjust in him to imprison his debtor during the whole period of his natural life. This would be an act of the most palpable injustice. But would the act of imprisonment become an act of justice if the debtor were, in the face of the payment, sent to prison even for a single hour? You can, every one of you, understand this, so as to affirm, without hesitation, that the circumstance of time does not change the moral character of the act. If it is right to condemn and imprison the man for one hour, it is not wrong, in the face of the payment, to condemn and imprison him for life; and, contrariwise, if it be wrong, in the face of the payment of the debt, to condemn and imprison him during life, it does not become right when the period of condemnation is indefinitely shortened. The injustice consists in the act of condemnation and imprisonment in the face of the payment, and not in the time during which the man has been sent to prison, or the place where he has been confined.

Let this illustration be applied to the case before us. It is said that God is bound in justice to justify all those for whom Christ died, and that he would act unjustly if he were to condemn them. The question is, Does he never condemn them? The question is not, Where does he condemn? or, How long does he condemn? The simple question which I press upon your notice is, Does God never at any time condemn them, in the face of the fact, that his Son has met the condemnation in their room and stead? Listen to what Jesus says, "He that believeth not is condemned already." It cannot, therefore, be unjust in God to condemn those for whom Christ has died. And hence it follows, as an inevitable conclusion, that their justification is not an act of justice but an act of grace.

What then becomes of John Calvin's doctrine of election? That doctrine, as we have seen, is based upon the assumption, that it is unjust in God, under any circumstances, to condemn any for whom the Saviour died. I appeal from Calvin and Candlish and the Confession of Faith, to the Word of God; and I ask you, with your Bibles, and the judgment-seat of God before you, solemnly to say, whether the doctrine, now under review, be not opposed to the word of truth and totally subversive of the grace of God in the salvation of the sinner.

But this is not all the mischief which results from the error now under consideration. That theory of election not only subverts the doctrine of free grace, it makes Jesus Christ himself the great agent in the overthrow. By this, the death of the Son of God is represented as instrumental in robbing the Father of his glory in the salvation of man. It is said that the sacrifice of his Son has rendered it imperative upon the Father to save certain sinners of the human race. This is an obligation binding upon God, in consequence of the atonement. Had Jesus not shed his blood for them, God would not have been bound in justice to save those sinners for whom he died. But now that his Son has died, it would be unjust in God to condemn them. This is what many people are taught to believe. Let us see to what an awful conclusion this statement conducts us.

It lands us at once in the conclusion, that by his atoning sacrifice, Jesus Christ has rendered it impossible for God to exercise grace in the justification of the sinner who believes. You will observe again, that we restrict our observation to the act of God in justifying the ungodly. We are not speaking of the previous act of God in giving up his Son to die, for it is but justice to those from whom we differ again to remind you, that their doctrine is free from the charge now advanced against it, if we confine ourselves merely to the act of the Father in giving up his Son to die for sinners. Our friends, from whom we differ, do not deny the grace of God in the primary act, of giving up his Son even to the death—the cursed death of the cross. They admit, and constantly do they affirm, that there is here the most wonderful manifestation of free grace the universe ever witnessed. And they are ever forward to make this most important and truthful concession. But you are not to permit your minds to be led off from the point now before us, by this admission on the part of Calvinists, important as it is. There is a difference between the act of God in sending his Son, and the act of God in justifying the ungodly who believe. The two acts of God are separate and distinct. The Son was sent into the world eighteen hundred years ago. The sinner who trusts to the sacrifice of the Son is not justified until he believes. You will observe, therefore, what is the precise charge which we adduce against that theory of election which restricts the death of Christ to the elect and to them alone. We affirm, that while it does not fail to exhibit the grace of God in the gift of his Son, it destroys the grace of God in the justification and salvation of the sinner; and, more especially, it exhibits the very sacrifice of the Son of God as that which renders it utterly impossible for God to exercise grace in the act of justification. If justification be of debt, it is no more of grace, otherwise debt is no more debt,—and if it be of grace, it is no more of debt, otherwise grace is no more grace. It matters not to whom it is affirmed, that God is bound, or to whom he is so indebted as to be compelled, in justice, to justify any sinner, be that sinner who he may. It matters not, though it should be said, as said it is, that God is bound or indebted, not as an act of justice to the sinner, but as an act of justice to his Son, to justify every sinner for whom he died. The merest child will perceive that this attempt to escape the dreadful conclusion is a mere evasion. For the question before us is not—to whom is God the Father bound. The simple query before us relates to the plain matter of fact—Is God bound, or is he free, to justify? If he be bound so that it would be unjust in him to condemn the sinner, it does not meet, but rather evades and jinks the difficulty, to turn our attention to the statement, that it is to his own Son that God is bound. Nothing can be more evident than this, that whether it be the sinner himself who has brought God under a debt of justice, or whether it be the sinner's substitute who has brought God under a debt of justice to justify the ungodly, the matter of fact is not thereby altered, but remains unchangeably the same, that on either supposition it is not justification by free grace, but justification as an act of common and ordinary justice which this notion of election ascribes to God the Father. What would you do, if any of you were owing me a debt of one thousand pounds, in order to destroy the possibility of any exercise of grace on my part? You would pay down the money. You would count it over to the uttermost farthing, and you would thereby evince your determination to put it out of my power to show you any favour—to exercise toward you any grace. And if you could not pay me yourself, in what other way could I be prevented from exercising toward you the slightest particle of grace? Your cautioner would pay down the money and forthwith demand your discharge. In this case, indeed, I would be shut up to the exercise of justice, but just for that reason would I be shut out from the barest possibility of exercising the prerogative of grace. The man would rob me of the honour or the glory of free grace by the self-same act, whereby he should constrain me to give you a discharge as an act of common honesty and ordinary justice.

Now it is precisely in this way that the Calvinian theory of election represents the Son of God as, by his very death, robbing his Father of the glory of his grace in the act of justifying the sinner who believes. It represents the Son as placing God under an obligation of strict justice thus to act. According to this, Jesus by his death left no room or scope whatever for the exercise of grace in the matter of justification. He thereby rendered the exercise of grace a natural and total impossibility. Such a representation, or rather misrepresentation, of the death of the Son of God, ought to be rejected, therefore, on account of "its excluding"—to quote again the well chosen words of the venerable Dr. Wardlaw—"everything of the nature of grace from every part of the process of the sinner's salvation excepting the original appointment of the surety, whose payment in each case of the estimated debt cancels the bond, and renders the liberation of the debtor not gracious but obligatory." Such is our deliberate assertion in reference to the scheme of doctrine now under examination. It is a tremendous charge which is substantiated against it, that it excludes everything of the nature of grace, and renders the justification of the sinner not gracious but obligatory.

And what renders the blasphemy more striking is the fact to which we now particularly advert. It represents the blessed atonement as putting an extinguisher upon the most glorious manifestation of the divine character. It exhibits the Son of God as playing the part of an unnatural Absalom, and tearing rudely from his father's crown the brightest gem which sparkles there. How widely different from all this is the real state of matters as exhibited in the Bible! Here we learn, that it was to honour his Father that the Son of God came down to earth upon his bloody and merciful errand. He came—not to destroy the possibility of his Father exercising the glorious prerogative of grace, but to open up a way for its wide and consistent manifestation. He came—not to shroud the free grace of God in everlasting gloom (a gloom illumined by no other manifestation save the fiery flash of justice), but to take away the covering which, but for his death, must ever have intervened between the grace of God and sinful man. He came—not to force a God of justice to save, but to leave God at liberty to save, without the slightest violation of one solitary principle of his righteous and just administration. He came—not for the purpose of fixing down upon his Father's character the charge of injustice, should his Father not extend to sinners the sceptre of mercy, and hold out the olive branch of peace—but to clear at once and for ever the injured and maligned reputation of God, by causing grace to walk forth over the sinful world (which the foul calumniator of God had said God did not love) in glorious harmony with justice and righteousness and truth. He came—not to make God out to be an unjust God if he should in any case not be received as a Saviour, but to exhibit God as a just God and yet a Saviour. He came—not to exhibit truth at the expense of mercy, nor righteousness at the expense of peace, but at his coming, and around his cross, "Mercy and truth met together, righteousness and peace embraced each other." In one single word, the death of Jesus did not render it imperative on God to save one sinner of the race. What then did it do? It rendered it consistent with the justice of God to save all who believe. In this way the blessed atonement did not destroy grace, but on the contrary it opened up a channel for its consistent exercise, so that now the whole world is under its benignant reign. And thus it is abundantly manifest, that while the coffin and the funeral and the grave-yard proclaim through all the earth, in the ears of all earth's generations, that "sin hath reigned unto death"—the rain and the sunlight and the healthful breeze, and above all, the lively hope of a blissful immortality, proclaim aloud to all, that "grace hath reigned through righteousness, unto eternal life, by Jesus Christ our Lord."

"Sin is frequently described as a debt (remarks Dr. Payne), and the atonement as the payment of this debt; and if we were careful to recollect that these are symbolical or figurative terms, we should not be misled by the phraseology. But the misfortune is, that words which are really figurative, and which are employed for the sole purpose of illustration, have been understood and explained literally. Sin has been represented as a real debt, and the atonement as a real payment of that debt; and the unhappy result is, that darkness of the densest kind has been made to envelope the whole subject. There are individuals who imagine that Christ rescues his people from the claims of divine justice in precisely the same way in which a generous friend delivers a debtor from captivity, by advancing the necessary sum in his behalf. Now I would not affirm that it is impossible for such persons to be saved by an humble hope in the mercy of God through Jesus Christ; but I can have no hesitation in expressing the opinion, that they do not understand the atonement.* A pecuniary satisfaction, and a moral satisfaction differ essentially in their nature, and proceed on radically different principles. Perhaps no man has set this difference in a clearer light than the late Mr. Fuller, whose words I quote:—'I apprehend,' says this excellent writer, 'that very important mistakes have arisen from considering the interposition of Christ under the notion of paying a debt. The blood of Christ is, indeed, the price of our redemption, or that for the sake of which we are delivered from the curse of the law; but this metaphorical language, as well as that of head and members, may be carried too far, and may lead us into many errors. In cases of debt and credit

* Dr. Payne does not surely suppose that any man can be saved who does not BELIEVE in the atonement. But Dr. P. has unanswerably proved that "*faith cannot exist where the meaning of the atonement is not understood.*"—Lec. 17, pp. 273, 274. How then CAN the persons referred to above be saved?

among men, when a surety undertakes to represent the debtor, from the moment his undertaking is accepted, the debtor is free, and may obtain his liberty, not as a matter of favour, at least on the part of the creditor, but of strict justice.' 'But who in his sober senses will imagine this to be analogous to the redemption of sinners by Jesus Christ? Sin is a debt only in a metaphorical sense; properly speaking, it is a crime, and satisfaction for it requires to be made, not on pecuniary, but on moral principles. If Philemon had accepted of that part of Paul's offer which respected property, and had placed so much of it to his account as he considered Onesimus to have owed him, he could not have been said to have remitted his debt, nor would Onesimus have had to thank him for remitting it. But it is supposed of Onesimus, that he might not only be in debt to his master, but have wronged him. Perhaps he had embezzled his goods, corrupted his children, or injured his character. Now, for Philemon to accept that part of the offer were very different from the other. In the one case, he would have accepted of a pecuniary representative; in the other, of a moral one; *i. e.*, of a mediator. The satisfaction, in the one case, would annihilate the very idea of remission; but not in the other. Whatever satisfaction Paul might give to Philemon respecting the wound inflicted upon his character and honour, as the head of a family, it would not supersede the necessity of pardon being sought by the offender, and freely bestowed by the offended.

"'The reason of this difference is easily perceived.

Debts are transferable, but crimes are not. A third person may cancel the one, but he can only obliterate the effects of the other; the desert of the criminal remains. The debtor is accountable to his creditor as a private individual, who has power to accept of a surety, or, if he please, to remit the whole without any satisfaction. In the one case he would be just, in the other merciful; but no place is afforded by either of them for the combination of justice and mercy in the same proceeding. The criminal, on the other hand, is amenable to the magistrate, or to the head of a family, as a public person; and who, especially if the offence be capital, cannot remit the punishment without invading law and justice; nor in the ordinary discharge of his office, admit of a third person to stand in his place. In extraordinary cases, however, extraordinary expedients are resorted to. A satisfaction may be made to law and justice, as to the spirit of them, while the letter is dispensed with. The well-known story of Zaleuchus, the Grecian lawgiver, who consented to lose one of his own eyes, to save one of his son's eyes—who, by transgressing the law, had subjected himself to the loss of both—is an example. Here, as far as it went, justice and mercy were combined in the same act; and had the satisfaction been much fuller than it was—so full that the authority of the law, instead of being weakened, should have been abundantly magnified and honoured, still it had been perfectly consistent with free forgiveness. Finally, in the case of the debtor, satisfaction being once accepted, justice requires his complete discharge; but in that of the criminal, where satisfaction is made to the wounded honour of the law and the authority of the lawgiver, justice, though it admits of his discharge, yet no otherwise requires it, than as it may have been matter of promise to the substitute.'"—*Payne on Sovereignty*, pp. 142–5.

This concluding observation, quoted by Dr. Payne from Andrew Fuller, unhappily clouds and obscures the whole of the valuable remarks which we have quoted in illustration of the point we have throughout been considering. It seems to indicate that the pardon of the sinner may, in one sense, be regarded as founded on a claim of justice, on the ground of a promise to the substitute. What is the promise, on the ground of which pardon is here supposed to be, in any sense, a matter of justice? and where is it to be found? Can any man point to a single promise made to our glorious substitute, wherein God binds himself to pardon any sinner as a matter of right? Where or when did the Father stipulate with the Son to dispense forgiveness to the believer on the presentation of a claim of justice? This is what the theory we are now considering, and the mistake against which Fuller was writing, most erroneously assumes. It assumes that the death of Jesus was of the nature of a pecuniary transaction—a pounds-shillings-and-pence satisfaction—on the ground of which, God could not fail to pardon all for whom it was offered, without being unjust. If this be a true representation of the death of the Son of God, the promise to dispense pardon, on the ground of it, could not be anything more or less than a promise to dispense a pardon which it would be unjust to withhold. But the extract just quoted points out the radical error which leads to such a view of the atonement; and our previous observations point out the fact, that the theory of election, which is based upon it, involves the subversion of free and sovereign grace. Now every blessing included in the promises of God to believers, God has pledged himself to communicate, not as an act of justice, but an act of grace. If then the promise itself involve a pledge to communicate blessings to the believing sinner, under the distinct provision that they might, every one of them, be righteously and justly withheld, it seems strange that any man should dream of founding upon such a promise a claim of justice and of right. We humbly submit, in opposition to the exceptionable statement on which we now remark, that even in the view of the promise, justice cannot require the release of the sinner who believeth in Jesus. This fact is certified by the very nature of the promise itself. It is the promise of pardon from a God, who, while he promises to pardon, promises also to retain and assert his right to condemn. It is a promise to dispense grace—free grace; and should any sinner lay hold of the promise, and seek to convert it into a claim of right, he thereby forfeits and rejects the very blessing which the Faithful and True Witness has pledged himself graciously to communicate. In the view of the promises, the sinner may, indeed, plead the FAITHFUL

NESS of a promise-loving and a promise-keeping God; but woe be to the man who perverts the grace of God, and the gracious promises of God, so as to imagine that, in any case, strict JUSTICE demands his release.

It is worthy of passing observation, that the doctrine we are engaged in examining is, in its bearing upon the grace of God, the twin sister of Socinianism. The Socinian denies altogether the necessity of a satisfaction for sin in order to warrant God to show mercy and extend his grace to the sinner. He leaves no room for the exercise of grace, because he points the sinner to no atonement for the satisfaction of the justice and the vindication of the righteousness of Jehovah. He thereby renders the exercise of grace an utter impossibility. But extremes meet. And so the system of Calvin and Candlish, by pursuing a different route around the circle of error, lands men in the self-same unscriptural and false conclusion. The latter system destroys grace by ascribing to justice the justification of the sinner; while the former system destroys grace by leaving no room for its consistent development. The Calvinist exclaims, that God would act unjustly if he did not justify. The Socinian rejoins, that no satisfaction has ever been made at all to divine justice. The one sets aside grace by ascribing the result to justice; the other sets aside grace, by leaving the sword of justice still unsheathed, so as still to guard and barup the way against the possibility of a free—a gracious salvation. Both systems agree in denying the free grace of God, and, therefore, both are proved to be utterly at variance with the Scriptures of truth.

Here, again, therefore, you perceive the application of the great principle exhibited at the outset of this discourse. And remembering the important distinction between what is above reason, and what is contrary to reason, you will be able, each one of you, freely to investigate, and candidly to decide. You will see that it is not with something plainly and distinctly revealed, but which is mysterious and concealed in its nature and bearings, that you have here to do. It is not with something above and beyond the reach of human reason to comprehend. We have here to do with a doctrine which is evidently absurd and false, because it is at once self-contradictory, and opposed to, and condemned by, the plainest doctrines of God's Word. It is utterly impossible for any man to believe two opposing statements at one and the same instant of time. He must cease to exercise his reason, and his common sense, if he can possibly be prevailed upon so to do. He must become a Papist, and hand over his conscience and his right of private judgment to the infallible Church, before he can possibly receive two contradictory statements as truth. The question, therefore, is level to the meanest capacity, and it is right that I should press it: Are you, my brethren, prepared to deny, and to cast aside, and to trample under foot, the free grace of God, and to perpetuate, as far as in you lies, the reign of error in our land, rather than cast away the doctrine which we have proved to be totally subversive of free grace? This is the simple question which we leave you to answer, every one of you, according to your responsibility to God, and not to man.

But ere I close my present address, suffer me, beloved friends, to approach a little more closely to the personal experience of each individual sinner in this assembly. May I not speak to each man amongst you, even as one friend addresses another, in sweet and familiar intercourse, and inquire of each of you, personally and individually—Hast thou tasted that the Lord is gracious? Canst thou not, my brother, honestly trust the heart of thy God? Wouldst thou bind HIM down with covenants and bonds, so that thou canst not feel thyself safe in his hands, unless thou canst defy him to hurt a hair of thine head by a desperate appeal to iron-handed justice? Wilt thou not trust his grace? Is it not enough, that the justice of God is fully and for ever satisfied for all thy sins, so that justice no longer bars the door against thy speedy, instant return to thy forsaken home of everlasting safety, and thy Father's bosom of infinite compassion? Wilt thou not think thyself safe enough in His presence, unless thou art assured that his hand is bound down by justice, so that he dare not smite thee for thy sins? Whence arises all this doubt? Whence all this fearful suspicion and trembling dread? Whence the anxious surmise that thy guilty soul is lost for ever, unless the God against whom thou hast rebelled, be bound in justice and in equity to save thee? Ah, my brother, seest thou not that all this is the work of the slanderer of thy God? "He loves thee not. He is a stern, relentless, heartless spirit. And withal he is omnipotent, and it is not safe for thee to trust him, unless thou seest him bound and shackled so that he cannot, dare not strike thee down." These are the suggestions of Satan, wherewith he would fill thy soul, O sinner, with unbelieving doubts and dark suspicions. "Behold the Lamb of God." Why did God give up his Son to die for all the world, and for thee? It was because he "so loved the world." His love, then, was not won or purchased by the wondrous sacrifice. His love to thy soul procured the sacrifice, and did not grudge the mighty cost whereby the flaming sword of angry justice might be averted from the gate which leads back to life and happiness for ever. Canst thou not, then, in the view of all this, trust the grace—the heart of thy God? Canst thou not trust that heart which loved thee so as to spare not his own Son? Canst thou not trust that heart which was pierced for thy sins upon the cross? Thy sins are all atoned for now. They form no reason why thou shouldst perish for ever. Thy Saviour's blood has washed them all away. But if in the face of all this, thou wilt still nourish thy damning unbelief, and hug to thy bosom a dark suspicion of thy God,—if thou wilt not cast aside thy doubts and fears until thou canst prevail upon thy trembling soul to think that thy God is bound, by an invincible necessity of justice and rectitude, to save thee,—if thou wilt not enter into heaven itself until thou canst read thy warrant, inscribed by the hand of justice over its shining portals —never—never—never canst thou enter in.

"Man, on the dubious waves of error toss'd,
His ship half-founder'd and his compass lost,
Sees, far as human optics may command,
A sleeping fog, and fancies it dry land;
Spreads all his canvas, every sinew plies;
Pants for't, aims at it, enters it, and dies!
Then farewell all self-satisfying schemes,
His well-built systems, philosophic dreams;
Deceitful views of future bliss, farewell!—
He reads his sentence at the flames of hell.
  Hard lot of man—to toil for the reward
Of virtue, and yet lose it! Wherefore hard?
He that would win the race must guide his horse
Obedient to the customs of the course;
Else, though unequall'd to the goal he flies,
A meaner than himself shall gain the prize.
GRACE LEADS THE RIGHT WAY: if you choose the wrong,
Take it and perish; but restrain your tongue;
Charge not, with light sufficient and LEFT FREE,
Your wilful suicide on GOD'S DECREE."

LECTURE THIRD.

CALVINISM AN INSIDIOUS SYSTEM—INCONSISTENT WITH THE FOREKNOWLEDGE, OPPOSED TO THE WISDOM, AND SUBVERSIVE OF THE HOLINESS OF JEHOVAH—DESTRUCTIVE OF HUMAN RESPONSIBILITY.

ISAIAH xlii. 9.—"Behold, the former things are come to pass, and new things do I declare: before they spring forth I tell you of them."

ISAIAH vi. 3.—"Holy, holy, holy is the Lord of Hosts."

JAMES i. 13.—"Let no man say, when he is tempted, I am tempted of God.

THE system which we are engaged now in examining, like every other system of error, is, in many respects, very like the truth. But for this circumstance, it is impossible to conceive how it could meet with any countenance at all from Christian men. It is not, however, without very high-sounding professions of consistency with, and attachment to, the Word of God; and it adapts itself so cunningly and artfully to the language of Scripture, that it seems at first sight, and without a very careful and sifting examination, to be in no respect whatever inconsistent with the revealed mind of God. You will accordingly observe that the leading abettors of this system begin to wax very furious and indignant whenever we venture to intimate the slightest suspicion of the soundness of their creed. It is thus, however, with every counterfeit. The base coin would not pass current at all unless it bore a very striking resemblance to the genuine gold. The forgery would never answer its end unless it was very like the real signature. And were it not for the single fact, that the system of theology which we oppose does retain in plentiful abundance, and exhibit in bold relief, much of THE PHRASEOLOGY of Scripture, its real character would be instantly detected, and it would stand out exposed before the eyes of men. It is in the shape of an angel of light that the destroyer of the souls of men for the most part appears. And it is under the character and pretensions of a system of Bible truth that Calvinism makes its advances among the children of men. There is, accordingly, a wonderful TALKING about free grace and gospel tidings and divine sovereignty and human depravity, and such like important doctrines, among the abettors of this system. So manifest is this fact, that the simple and guileless multitude of men and women who are imposed upon by mere appearances, are very naturally shocked and disgusted whenever they hear it faithfully announced, that the system whereby they are verily deceived and imposed upon is really and truly a subverter of those precious truths which it professes to respect. The name of truth is, indeed, retained, but the thing signified by the name, even Truth herself, has been banished from the system. And were it not that the lovers of truth delight in listening to the very mention of her name, and never dream of suspecting, or so much as examining minutely into the real character of the Confession of Faith, and do find in THE BIBLE what they would never discover in THE CREED, it would not be possible to find one solitary Christian man prepared to stake his Christian reputation, side by side, with the system of which we speak. It is a relief to the mind which contemplates this horrid system of delusion to reflect, even for an instant, upon the circumstance to which we now advert. Many of the abettors of Calvinism are really ignorant of the system which they unhappily patronize: "they know not what they do;" "they themselves are saved, so as by fire." But while such persons are really angry with us when they listen for the first time to the grave and heavy charges which we advance against their system, "they do not well to be angry." And we should do no better if we were deterred, either by the disapprobation of good men, who are imposed upon by the mere pretensions of a theology which they have never examined, or by the impotent rage and calumnious aspersions of bad men, who know full well that the system cannot stand examination, and spend their strength in deceitful attempts to patch and paint the idol whereby precious souls are ruined: if either by the frown of the one or the fury of the other, we were deterred from faithfully and affectionately warning you and your children of your danger, we should be verily guilty of our brother's blood. We do not calumniate the system we oppose; we ourselves were many a long year deceived by it, and at the expense of the disruption of many a tie dear to flesh and blood, we have come out from its fatal and contaminating influence. We call upon you, our brethren, to "come out and be separate, and touch not the unclean thing." He is the calumniator who lifts his voice and wields his influence against a truth which he has never examined or brought to the test of the Word of God, but which he ignorantly stigmatizes by the name of heresy. We ask no more from any man among you than an examination of what is said to be true. If it be truth, it cannot suffer from the most searching scrutiny. And whoever he be who would dissuade or deter you, or himself shrink back from openly and honestly bringing his system of theology to the test of the Word of God, thereby betrays an innate consciousness of its weakness. While it is, therefore, a relief to the mind to believe that many of the adherents of this system are the children of God, it is unspeakably painful to think that any of the children of God should continue to countenance the system. They are betrayed, as we have said, by ignorance of the true character of what they sinfully uphold. They are seduced by mere pretensions. They are charmed away by a pleasing sound. No phrase is more frequently exhibited by this theology than FREE GRACE; but we have seen in our former Lecture that while the name is not taken away, the system we oppose destroys the thing itself, and really subverts the grace of God in the justification of the sinner who believes.

We are about to call your attention this evening to another example of the perfidiousness and treachery of Calvinism. This system professes to be very zealous for the character of God, and more particularly does it profess to vindicate and uphold the great Bible doctrine respecting the FOREKNOWLEDGE, the WISDOM, and the HOLINESS of Jehovah. If it failed to exhibit this profession, the eyes of good men would at once be open to its true character, and it would instantly lose the influence which it exerts by virtue of its Christian name and its high religious pretensions. But we hope this evening to convince you, that the doctrine of Calvin and the Confession is really subversive of the divine foreknowledge as well as inconsistent with the wisdom and holiness of the Godhead.

IV. THE FOURTH OBJECTION WHICH WE NOW ADDUCE AGAINST THE THEORY UNDER CONSIDERATION, ARISES FROM ITS INCONSISTENCY WITH THE DIVINE FOREKNOWLEDGE.

When we speak of foreknowledge, we use a word which is familiar to you all. It may not be unnecessary, however, to anticipate and guard against prevalent misconceptions, by calling your attention, in this place, to one or two simple explanations. It will be observed, therefore, (1,) that foreknowledge implies, in every instance, the FUTURE and CERTAIN existence of the object known or apprehended by the mind. It is not FORE or before-hand knowledge if the object known or apprehended have a present or a past existence; and it is not KNOWLEDGE at all if there be any doubt or uncertainty in reference to the existence of the object apprehended, whether we conceive that object to be past or present or future in relation to the intelligence which apprehends it. There may be conjecture or guesswork where there is something less than positive certainty, but without certainty there can be no knowledge. You will notice, farther, in this connexion, (2,) that knowledge is something which is necessarily and invariably present in relation to the intelligence of whom such knowledge can be truthfully and invariably predicated. If it can be truly and invariably said of any being that "HE KNOWS," it is evident that the knowledge is invariably present whether the object of knowledge or the thing known be removed from him by space or by time —whether it be distant or future or past. The knowledge or act of the mind in knowing is always a present act, wherever the knowledge exists and by whomsoever it is possessed. My friend may be far *distant* from me, but the knowledge which I possess of his excellences is *present;* distance of time or place does not and cannot affect the knowledge itself, which can neither be past nor future nor distant, but, wherever it exists at all, exists necessarily as a PRESENT KNOWLEDGE. You will notice, (3,) that it is not the knowledge which originates the certainty, but the reverse. An event is not certain because it is known; it comes within the sphere of knowledge because it is certain. The knowledge of any event, whether past, present, or future, does not affect its certainty: it is known because it is certain. The cause of its existence must be sought elsewhere than in the knowledge whether fore or after. Foreknowledge does not, any more than after knowledge, define or certify anything as to THE CAUSE OR ORIGIN OF THE OBJECT apprehended by the mind.

You will observe the importance of such explanations, the oversight of which lies at the foundation of much error and misconception on the subject now under consideration. Of this you may be convinced by a mere passing reference to a very popular and threadbare story, which is, no doubt, regarded as a conclusive demonstration by modern Calvinistic divines. It is related in the form of a conversation which is said to have taken place between a certain Independent minister and a fellow-traveller who strongly objected to the Calvinistic decrees.

"I would ask," said the minister, "is the great God under any necessity of waiting till the last day in order to determine who are the righteous that are to be saved, and the wicked who are to perish?"

"By no means," said the other, "for he certainly knows already."

"When do you imagine," asked the minister, "that he first attained this knowledge?" Here the gentleman paused, and hesitated a little; but soon answered, "He must have known from all eternity."

"Then," said the minister, "it must have been fixed from all eternity."

"That by no means follows," replied the other.

"Then it follows," added the minister, "that he did not *know* from all eternity, but only *guessed*, and happened to guess right; for how can Omniscience *know* what is yet uncertain?"

Here the gentleman began to perceive his difficulty, and, after a short debate, confessed it should seem it must have been fixed from eternity.

"Now," said the minister, "one question more will prove that you believe in predestination as well as I. You have acknowledged what can never be disproved, that God could not know from eternity who shall be saved unless it had been fixed from eternity. If then, it was fixed, be pleased, sir, to inform me who fixed it?"—*Quoted in Bonar's "Truth and Error,"* pp. 61, 62.

The gentleman is here said, as the story goes, to have acknowledged he had never taken this view of the subject before, and to have promised on the spot never more to speak against John Calvin or his decrees.

You have here a specimen of a class of very ignorant or very crafty ministers on the one hand, and of very simple and very thoughtless gentlemen on the other. Both parties evidently overlooked the fact, that KNOWLEDGE defines nothing whatever respecting THE CAUSE of the event known. Knowledge, whether of a past or of a future event, apprehends the certain existence of whatever it apprehends at all, but it does not cause or originate the existence of anything whatever. But both the minister and the gentleman failed to observe this fact, and so they erroneously concluded that God's infallible knowledge of all events, involves, on his part, the necessary causation of all events, as if nothing whatever could be certainly foreknown unless it were certainly and absolutely decreed, or "fixed," by God himself. The gentleman was, therefore, confused and mystified by the gratuitous and false assumption, that unless God had himself unconditionally or absolutely "fixed" or decreed whatsoever comes to pass, he could not foreknow the certain existence of anything future, but "ONLY GUESSED, and happened to guess right." But if this gentleman had only considered what he unfortunately overlooked and misapprehended, he would have seen at once that the knowledge of any object, past, present, or future, does not call that object into existence, or render its existence certain. He would have seen the very opposite to be true. He would have seen that the knowledge of anything future presupposes and apprehends its certain future existence, no less evidently than the knowledge of any present or past event presupposes and apprehends its present or past existence, altogether independently of, or (it may even be) altogether opposed to, the will of the being who knows it. When our Saviour was upon the earth, he compassionately sought to convince his crafty antagonists by wisely saying unto them, "I also will ask of you one question" (Mark xi. 29), instead of replying directly to their leading queries, which were purposely framed to entrap and to ensnare him. And if this Christian gentleman had followed the example of his master, he would have replied to the very first question of the minister who led him into the snare, by proposing a question which would have "fixed" his reverend adversary. When the minister asked him, "Is the great God under any necessity of waiting till the last day IN ORDER TO KNOW who will be saved and who will be lost?" the gentleman would have done well to have said, "I also will ask of you one question—Is the great God under any necessity of himself causing and necessitating the commission of sin, 'IN ORDER TO KNOW' the sinful actions which shall be committed by devils and by wicked men?" Had such a question been kindly and respectfully proposed, we should very probably have heard nothing at all from Calvinists of the threadbare narrative which it has become fashionable to retail. Such a question as this would certainly have brought the minister to a stand, even as our Saviour's question "fixed" the Pharisees when he asked them, "The baptism of John, was it from heaven or of men?" The minister would very probably have paused and argued thus within himself:—"If I shall say that God is the primary cause of sinful actions, I fear the people, because they believe that 'THE LORD OUR GOD IS HOLY;' and if I shall say that God can foreknow any thing which he has not himself determined to bring to pass, he will say, 'Why then do you believe John Calvin's unscriptural creed?'"—and so, in all likelihood, the debate would have terminated.

But it is at this point that the inquiry ought to begin. The question is, whether it be not a blasphemy against God to maintain a creed which affirms plainly that, "for his own glory, God hath foreordained whatsoever comes to pass." Our opponents in this argument, have no right to hold that this question is to be decided simply on the faith of their false and blundering assertions. They have no right to assert and to take it for granted, without even an attempt at proof, that OMNISCIENCE is capable of doing no more than "GUESSING" after an event, unless OMNIPOTENCE be pledged to bring that event into being. We are entitled to demand the strongest PROOF in support of this important statement, and our friends who oppose us are not entitled to give us no more than bare ASSERTION in its support, as from the time of their sainted Augustine they have invariably done. We demand the evidence in support of the assertion on which Calvinism and Fatalism and Socialism are all of them based—the assertion that God himself is incapable of foreknowing things future, without previously resolving, by his Omnipotence, to bring them into existence.

On this point we have been absolutely deluged with assertion, but we look in vain for one particle of proof. It has been assumed, as if it were even an axiom, that whatever is UNDECREED by God is for that simple reason a thing UNCERTAIN, and to be fathered upon a nonentity which men call "CHANCE." You will notice therefore the importance of the simple facts which have been already submitted to your attention, and you will more particularly remember that the very idea of foreknowledge implies the idea of certainty, but the question remains still to be disposed of, whether it be true, as Calvinists assert, that God cannot foreknow future events, without first of all decreeing their certain existence, and then apprehending them through the medium of his own decree.

That such is the position maintained by Calvinists, is

evident from all their writings, from some of which I select now one or two quotations.

I call your attention, in the first place, to a single statement from their great master himself. John Calvin writes as follows, in the twenty-third chapter of the third book of his Institutes :—

"Since he [God] DOTH NOT OTHERWISE FORESEE the things that shall come to pass, than because he hath decreed that they should so come to pass, it is vain to move a controversy about foreknowledge where it is certain that all things do happen rather by ordinance and commandment. . . . . No man shall be able to deny but that God foreknew what end man should have, ere he created him, and THEREFORE FOREKNEW IT BECAUSE he had so ordained by his decree."—Sec. 6, 7.

Such are Calvin's own words, and you will notice that there are two separate and distinct statements contained therein, the first of which is admitted to be true, but the second of which is altogether false and unsupported in any place by the smallest shadow of evidence. The first statement asserts what no man denies—the foreknowledge of God. The second statement assumes what cannot be proved, and what no Calvinist, so far as we know, has ever attempted to establish by anything like proof, viz., that God does not foreknow anything he has not himself fixed by his own absolute and irreversible decree. But, unfortunately for Calvinism, it so happens that the very point which is universally taken for granted, is the precise point which needs to be unanswerably proved.

Jerom Zanchius, another distinguished Calvinist, writes as follows:—"God's foreknowledge, taken abstractedly, is not the sole cause of beings and events; but his will and foreknowledge together. Hence we find, Acts ii. 23, that his determinate council and foreknowledge act in concert; THE LATTER RESULTING FROM, AND BEING FOUNDED ON, THE FORMER. . . . . Consequently it is his free pleasure *to permit sin*, since, without his permission, neither men nor devils can do anything. Now, to *permit*, is, at least, the same as *not to hinder*, though it be in our power to hinder if we please; and this permission or non-hindrance is certainly an act of the Divine will. Hence, Austin says, 'Those things which seemingly thwart the Divine will are nevertheless agreeable to it; for if God did not permit them, they could not be done; and whatever God permits he permits freely and willingly. He does nothing, neither suffers anything to be done against his own will.' And Luther observes that 'God permitted Adam to fall into sin, because he willed that he should so fall.'"—*The Doctrine of Absolute Predestination, translated from the Latin of Zanchius, by Augustus Toplady, with Prefatory Essay by the late Dr. Pringle of the Secession Church, Perth*, pp. 39, 40.

This quotation proves not only that foreknowledge is held by the Calvinist to be founded on God's absolute decree, but it evinces still farther the important fact, that according to this theology the foreknowledge is really confounded with the decree altogether, inasmuch as it is in plain words spoken of as in connexion with the the decree, "THE POSITIVE CAUSE of all beings and events."

This wonderful mixture of truth and error is exhibited by Mr. Bonar of the Free Church, in his appropriately-named book. I quote the following extract from the fiftieth page of "TRUTH AND ERROR."

"It is of some importance [says Mr. Bonar] that we should settle the nature of these two things, predestination and foreknowledge, and ascertain which of the two is first. The question, is 'Does God fix a thing simply because he foreknows it, or does he foreknow it because he has fixed it?' . . . . I answer unhesitatingly, That PREDESTINATION MUST BE THE FOUNDATION of foreknowledge. God foreknows EVERYTHING THAT TAKES PLACE BECAUSE HE HAS FIXED IT."

We pause again to call your attention to the absurdity which Calvinists incessantly perpetrate by a sheer forgetfulness of the plain explanations to which we have formerly adverted. Mr. Bonar writes as if anything foreknown *needed to be subsequently fixed* by a decree of God, and he accordingly proposes the ridiculous question, "Does God fix a thing simply because he foreknows it?" He cannot conceive of anything as certain or foreseen as certain, unless it has been fixed unalterably by the almighty will of God! And so you will observe, that this writer gives us the benefit of his own simple assurance in common with that of his fellow Calvinists, that God first fixes and decrees to bring everything to pass; and then, and only then, is it possible for God to know beforehand anything that shall afterwards happen!

The only other quotation which I shall now make, is from the Lectures on Theology, which were delivered to the students of the Secession Church (now United Presbyterian), by the late Dr. Dick of Glasgow.

"No effect can be viewed as future [says this Professor], or, in human language, can be the object of certain expectation, but when considered in relation to its efficient cause; and the cause of all things which ever shall exist is the purpose of God, 'who worketh all things after the counsel of his own will.' As the knowledge of God does not depend upon the actual existence of objects—for this would limit it to the present and the past—so it does not depend upon any conditions attached to their existence. He does not know that such things shall happen, if such other things shall go before; but the whole series of events was planned by his infinite understanding, the ends as well as the means: and he foresees the ends, not through the medium of the means, but THROUGH THE MEDIUM OF HIS OWN DECREE, in which they have a certain future existence. They will not take place without the means, but THE PROPER cause of them is not the means, but his almighty will."—Vol. i. p. 384, *first edition.*

We add no more in this place in the shape of quotation, and we have detained you with such extracts, from ancient and modern authors, simply with the view of anticipating the charge of misrepresentation, which Calvinists are not slow to make whenever their dogmas happen to be subjected to a fair examination. It is better therefore to leave our friends to speak for themselves.

What then do you think of their creed? What is its evident bearing upon the foreknowledge of the Deity? Does it not reduce the attribute of omniscience to a mere name, and resolve it into a thing which is dependent upon, and subordinate to, the omnipotence of the Godhead? Does it not strip God of his peculiarly glorious distinction, as an ALL-SEEING Jehovah? And while this theology does retain the name, does it not set aside the reality, and represent God himself as reduced to the necessity of learning or acquiring the knowledge of futurity, exclusively from his present existing determinations and his present existing power? And is not this, properly speaking, a knowledge of something PRESENT, as much as of any thing future? When we speak of knowledge as INTUITIVE, we surely mean to express something very different from knowledge ACQUIRED through any medium whatever. And when we ascribe omniscience to the Deity, we surely mean to intimate something more than the possession, on his part, of a mere perception of what is his present will at any future time to bring assuredly to pass. Such a knowledge as this is possessed by the meanest of created intelligences. The question, therefore, resolves itself simply into this—"Whether the knowledge of God be, or be not, distinguished from that even of the highest of his creatures, by virtue not only of its extent, but more especially of its independence—its absolute independence, even of his own decrees." We humbly submit that this question must be answered in the affirmative, from the three following considerations:—Consider (1) the innate and infinite perfection of the Divine intelligence, and say whether omniscience needs to derive its information through any conceivable medium. Consider (2) the infinite purity of the Divine nature, and say whether sin and every abominable thing which exists, could possibly find its origin and cause in the mind of a holy God—a supposition involved necessarily in the hypothesis, that God needed first to decree in order that he might be able to foreknow whatsoever comes to pass. Consider (3) the direct and explicit language of Scripture, wherein the decree of God is exhibited as consequent upon his foreknowledge, which is a plain contradiction of the theory that his foreknowledge is dependent upon his decree. It is written, for example, in Rom. viii. 29, "Whom he did FOREKNOW, he also did PREDESTINATE;" and in 1 Peter i. 2, "Elect ACCORDING TO the foreknowledge of God." In such like statements of the inspired record, the foreknowledge is in the order of nature prior to the decree.

We say not only that Calvinism is UN-scriptural, based as it is upon a gratuitous assumption which derives no warrant from the Word of God; but we are entitled to denounce this figment of man's imagination as ANTI-scriptural, inasmuch as it is founded entirely upon the monstrous conception, that nothing whatever could possibly be certainly apprehended, even by the Divine mind, save through the medium of a horrible and demon-like decree. And more especially do we now call your attention to the fact, that the true and proper foreknowledge of the Deity (by which we mean his independent and intuitive apprehension of all things actual and all things possible—of all things future as well as of all that is past or present) is blasphemously denied by the theory now under consideration. This theory degrades the Godhead beneath the level of many of his creatures. Whatever any sinful creature possesses the power to do, and resolves to carry into execution, the creature must of necessity foreknow. Grant ye that he has the will to act, and that he possesses in addition to the will, the power to carry his purpose into execution, and the basest of the fallen intelligences must needs be able, with infallible certainty, to predict the result. But there is nothing peculiar—nothing wonderful in any sinful mortal claiming and possessing an attribute such as this. You may wonder at the man's power, or you may be astounded at the man's purpose to employ his power in any given direction, but you cannot wonder at the man's knowledge. He merely predicts or foretells what he has himself determined to carry into effect in the exercise, it may be, of his astonishing powers. Suppose that it is a deed of darkness which the man contemplates. He comes to you announcing, for example, that on some future day, and at a given hour, your friend will certainly die. You are astonished at the man's intelligence. You ask eagerly and anxiously how he happens to know the very day and hour when his fellow-mortal is to be ushered into eternity. But what if, at the hour and day appointed, you come to learn that the pretended prophet did himself determine to murder your friend with his own hand, and did acquire his foreknowledge through the medium of his own decree? Would you, in such a case, laud your informant as a very wonderful prophet? Would you not rather proclaim him a murderer—a cool, deliberate murderer—whose dire prediction was founded solely on his dire decree? In such a case the murderer has no claim whatever to the character of the prophet. It is not his foreknowledge, but his villany, of which you would speak. And in such a case it might well be questioned, if it be not an abuse of language to ascribe to him the attribute of foreknowledge at all. The reason is, that in such a case what the man knew was, properly speaking, his own dark and villanous intention, and his own abused and perverted power. But these were PRESENT at the time when the prediction was first announced, and it was through the medium of these alone that the murderer pried into the future, and so, strictly speaking, it was not so much the knowledge of the future event, as the knowledge of a present determination or purpose, which was intimated to you in the form of a prophecy. This is a revelation of a purpose already formed, which depends for its fulfilment merely on the will and power of the executioner, and forms of itself no proper exhibition of foreknowledge on the part of the individual who utters it.

Let this illustration be applied to the question now before us. It is said that the decree of God is the exclusive foundation of his foreknowledge. He is said to foreknow whatever shall come to pass, simply because he has himself resolved, by an act of his almighty will, to bring about whatsoever comes to pass. His knowledge, therefore, of the events of futurity is not anything more than a necessary existing consciousness of his present determination, coupled with a consciousness of his resistless power. It amounts to nothing more than a consciousness of what he himself has purposed, in the exercise of omnipotence, to bring about. And while it cannot be denied that all this may exalt the power of God, we hold it to be self-evident, that it strikes at the root of his omniscience, which involves, on his part, the independent or intuitive perception of all the thoughts and words and deeds of his free and intelligent and responsible creatures, and that too from the unbeginning ages of eternity.

This is the peculiar glory of God as an omniscient being. His peculiar glory consists in his knowing infallibly from all eternity the free volitions and actions of free and responsible agents who exist in time. This is what is fitted to strike the human mind with wonder and adoration. That God should know, with infallible certainty, all the thoughts and intents—all the purposes and doings, of all the generations of men before men came into being! That is the wonder. And that forms the grand and striking peculiarity of the prophetic announcements contained in the blessed Bible, which being fulfilled to the very letter, in the history of the human race, have, in every age, manifested the book wherein they are contained, to be emphatically THE BOOK OF GOD.

While, therefore, there exists not a creature, however ignorant or vile, who does not know, of necessity, beforehand, whatever he has the will and the power himself to execute, and who may not, in every such case, predict the result with infallible certainty,—while the most debased of created intelligences is possessed of foreknowledge such as this, where is the man or the angel, however exalted in intellect or knowledge, who can predict, with infallible certainty, what shall be the volitions and actions of moral and intelligent agents, upon whose minds no irresistible force is exercised, but WHO ARE FREE to think and act, to choose or to refuse, as each shall independently determine? This is something which the Bible assures us belongs only to God. This is an achievement so truly marvellous, and so far beyond the reach of men, that no man can tell how it comes to pass. Here is something ABOVE reason, and here we have an apt illustration and example of the principle adverted to at the outset of our last Sabbath evening lecture, in reference to what is above reason as distinguished from what is contrary to reason. There is nothing here to shock our reason. There are no such palpable contradictions as are to be found everywhere in Calvinism for men to gulp down—there is no contradiction at all in this glorious truth. And though it be far above the reach of the human mind to scrutinize the HOW and the WHEREFORE—though no man nor angel can say, how it is or wherefore it is—we have here something which exalts the Godhead in our conceptions, and which constrains us to wonder and to adore. "Canst thou by searching find out God? Canst thou find out the Almighty unto perfection? It is high as heaven, what canst thou do? deeper than hell, what canst thou know? The measure thereof is longer than the earth, and broader than the sea." Job xi. 7–9. The disciple of Calvin tells us that HE, forsooth! cannot understand how God can possibly foreknow whatsoever comes to pass, unless it be that God has fixed, by his decree, every abomination that takes place under the sun, and has determined himself to bring it about. And what does the self-blinded devotee presume to do? He presumes to measure the mind of God by his own puny intellect, and to affirm that God must have infallibly and unconditionally "foreordained whatsoever comes to pass." And why? Because short-sighted mortals cannot understand how God can foreknow anything as certain, or can do more than "GUESS" the existence of anything which God has not himself determined to bring into being! This is not only most unfair and inconclusive reasoning, if reasoning indeed it can be called, it is the framing of a man-made, arbitrary theory; it is pure speculation, and that, too, in direct opposition to the Word of God. What said the sweet singer of Israel? Did he deny such knowledge as this, because it was peculiar to God, and far too wonderful for his finite comprehension? Did he attempt to bring the subject of the Divine foreknowledge down to the level of his capacity by approaching the blundering, blasphemous conclusion, that GOD MUST have first resolved to exert his power in determining his downsitting and his uprising, and giving birth to his every wicked thought, and chalking out his every devious course—and then, and thus only, was enabled to know all that concerned him long before his thoughts came into existence? Such was not the mind of the inspired psalmist. "O Lord, thou hast searched me, and known me. Thou knowest my downsitting and mine uprising; thou understandest my thought afar off. Thou compassest my path, and my lying down, and art acquainted with all my ways. For there is not a word in my tongue, but, lo, O Lord, thou knowest it altogether. Thou hast beset me behind and before, and laid thine hand upon me." Psalm cxxxix. 1–5.

What, then, was the conclusion at which the psalmist arrived? Did he account for the circumstance, that God knew his thought afar off, on the Socialist principle, that God had decreed the existence of his every thought? Did he console himself under his iniquity by falling back upon the decree of God as the ultimate cause of it? Did he say that he could easily account for the foreknowledge of God by tracing that knowledge to a previous decree? No such thing. He immediately adds (verse 6), "SUCH KNOWLEDGE IS TOO WONDERFUL FOR ME; IT IS HIGH, I CANNOT ATTAIN UNTO IT." But such knowledge is not too high for the follower of Calvin! He can explain it all! He has a ready-made theory, whereby he can easily account for knowledge such as this! It is such knowledge as any creature can attain unto, even as every creature must necessarily foreknow the existence of what he has himself decreed! The Calvinist will not condescend to stoop down to the position occupied by the psalmist, but he at once rushes onward, in the pride of his system of theology, to the impious DENIAL of the Divine foreknowledge of every thought, word, and deed of men and devils, which God has not originated and foreordained! Horrible conclusion! Away with the theology which inculcates it! Such a theology is a wild dream of pagan philosophy, a delusion, and a falsehood from the father of lies, wherewith he practises a foul deception upon the souls of men!

We have already quoted an extract from Jerom Zanchius, translated by Toplady, and recommended by Dr. Pringle of the Secession, to the Scottish public. And as we have distinctly asserted that the doctrine of Calvin and the Confession of Faith is part and parcel of pagan philosophy, we here read to you the reply which Toplady gives to this very grave accusation, which has been long ago advanced against the theory now under review. In the fifteenth page of his preface, this writer meets the charge by indirectly admitting it:—

"But does not this doctrine tend [says he] to the establishment of FATALITY? Supposing it even did, were it not better to be a CHRISTIAN FATALIST than to avow a set of loose Arminian principles, which, if pushed to their natural extent, inevitably terminate in the rankest *Atheism?* For, without predestination there can be no Providence, and, without Providence, no God.

"After all, what do you mean by FATE? If you mean *a regular succession of determined events*, from the beginning to the end of time; *an uninterrupted chain*, without a single chasm; all *depending* on the eternal *will* and continued *influence* of the GREAT FIRST CAUSE; if *this is* Fate, it must be owned. . . .

"It having been not unusual, with the Arminian writers, to tax us with adopting THE FATE OF THE ANCIENT STOICS, I thought it might not be unacceptable to the *English* reader to subjoin a brief view of what those philosophers *generally* held (for they were not all exactly of a mind) as to this particular. It will appear to every competent reader, from what is there given, *how far* the doctrine of FATE, as believed and taught by the STOICS, may be admitted upon CHRISTIAN PRINCIPLES.* . . .

"For my own particular part [adds Toplady] I frankly confess that, as far as the coincidence of the STOICAL FATE with the Bible predestination holds good, I see no reason why we should be ashamed to acknowledge it. *St. Austin,* and many other great and excellent men, have not scrupled to admit both the word

* We also take the liberty of quoting, in our Appendix, this precious morsel of heathenism, from which the reader will see whence Calvinism has sprung—not from the Bible, but from the schools of pagan philosophy, Toplady himself being witness. See Appendix.

(viz., the word FATE) and THE THING, properly understood. I am quite of LIPSIUS'S mind, '*Et vero non aversabor* STOICI *nomen; sed* STOICI CHRISTIANI,' *i. e.*, I have no objection to be called a STOIC, so you but prefix the word CHRISTIAN to it."—*Preface to Zanchius on Predestination, by Toplady*, pp. 15–17.

Such, then, is an honest confession of a disciple of Calvin of no mean name. The system speaks for itself, and no man who looks it in the face but must see more of the pagan than of the Christian pervading its every feature. But as we live now in an age and country where many Calvinistic divines labour not to defend, but to conceal and hide, the abominable system from the eyes of the multitude, who still, in tears, follow it onward to the scaffold, it is necessary to hold it up before you as it has been stated and defended by a generation of less temporizing and more honest men. There is no need for weeping and bewailing the approaching destruction of this monstrous system. Let every Christian man and woman in this audience rejoice and give thanks to God, that the time has arrived when the great majority of professed Calvinists are ashamed of their idol, and are tacitly, at least, even now, consenting to its too tardy execution.

V. WE OBJECT TO THIS THEORY OF ELECTION, BECAUSE IT SUBVERTS THE WISDOM OF GOD IN HIS DECREES.

We take Dr. Dick's own definition of wisdom, as found in the Twenty-Second Lecture of his course. This author very truly says, "Wisdom cannot exist

8

without knowledge, but knowledge may exist without wisdom; and accordingly there are men possessing very extensive information who, in their conduct, give many proofs of thoughtlessness and folly. In an all-perfect being, they are necessarily conjoined, omniscience supplies the materials of infinite wisdom. As God knows all his creatures, all their powers and qualities, all the purposes to which they may be rendered subservient, all the relations in which they may be placed, and all the possible consequences of all possible events, he is able infallibly to determine what are the most proper ends to be pursued, and what are the fittest means of effecting them."

With these sentiments every one must agree. But you will observe their bearing upon the system now under review.

There can be no wisdom without knowledge going before it. And thus it is that WE argue out the wisdom of all God's purposes and decrees. They are most wise, because they are founded upon the foreknowledge of all the future volitions and actions of free agents who shall exist in time.

But Calvinism says that the foreknowledge of God is founded on his decrees. God knows whatever shall come to pass, in consequence of having already decreed whatever shall come to pass.

The decree of God is accordingly represented as independent of, and in the order of nature before, his knowledge.

Seeing, therefore, that there can be no wisdom without knowledge, the decrees of God cannot possibly be wise! Themselves the foundation of all knowledge in the mind of the Deity, they preceded all knowledge, and were formed ignorantly and blindly! Such is the predestination of Calvin. It is nothing more nor less than blind necessity—unadulterated fatalism. We proceed to notice,

VI. That this theory of election destroys all moral distinctions between right and wrong, good and evil; and thereby stands opposed to the holiness of God.

We have already seen that it traces every thing which takes place in the universe to the almighty will of God, as the efficient and primary cause of all. It is very often said, in so many words, by the supporters of Calvin, that God is not the cause of sin; but such a true saying, proceeding from Calvinists, is nothing more nor less than an idle and unmeaning and heartless compliment. Such a truthful announcement is contradicted by the system, and is a mere word of course. It reminds one of the traitor Judas, when he went up to Jesus and said, "Hail, Master, and kissed him." It is verily true that God is not the author of sin, but why should men cleave to a system of theology which represents God as the only originator and cause of all iniquity—a system which forces men to the conclusion that, in asserting the holiness of God, the Holy Spirit is studiously hiding and concealing the truth—a system which makes God the author of every abomination that ever was perpetrated among men? Does the Shorter Catechism make any exception when it says, that "God has foreordained WHATSOEVER comes to pass"? Does it not here trace everything, without exception, to the decree of God? Does it not teach babes and sucklings to say, that God has decreed every sinful action; and, in connexion with this, that "God executeth his decrees in the works of creation and providence"? Here is, first of all, every abomination fathered upon the decree of God; and here is, in the second place, God pointed out as the active executioner of the whole array of wickedness that comes to pass in the history of devils and of men! Here is, surely, "THE MYSTERY OF INIQUITY," which, even in apostolic times, had already begun to do its deadly work, and to emit its horrid blasphemies. Listen to another statement from Zanchius, from whom I have already quoted: "I would infer [says this writer, p. 63] that if we would maintain the doctrine of God's OMNIPOTENCE, we must insist upon that of his UNIVERSAL AGENCY; the *latter* cannot be denied without giving up the *former*. Disprove that he is almighty, and then we will grant that his influence and operations are limited and circumscribed. Luther says that God would not be a RESPECTABLE BEING, if he were not almighty, and THE DOER OF ALL THINGS THAT ARE DONE; or if anything could come to pass in which he had no hand."

In accordance with this doctrine, Mr. Bonar of the Free Church says, in "Truth and Error,"—"Nothing in the universe takes place without the will of God. This is admitted. But it is asked, Is this will *first* in everything? I answer, Yes. The will of God goes before all other wills. It does not depend on them, but they depend on it. ITS MOVEMENTS REGULATE THEM. The 'I will' of Jehovah is that which sets in motion everything in heaven and in earth. The 'I will' of Jehovah is the spring and origin of all that is done throughout the universe, great or small, among things animate or inanimate." P. 24.

It follows, naturally and necessarily, from this doctrine, that there is no distinction between good and evil, right and wrong, truth and error, sin and holiness! Everything is in accordance with the "I will" of Jehovah! His will must be right; and whatever is, is accordingly RIGHT—seeing that everything is in accordance with the will of God, who "would not be a respectable being," if he were not himself "the doer of all things that are done,"—devils and wicked men being only the passive tools in his almighty hand!!!

Said we not truly that we have here the full development of "the mystery of iniquity," bellowing forth her horrid blasphemies against God; and by her loud and specious pretensions of attachment to the Word of God, deceiving, "if it were possible, the very elect"? The upholders of this system make an attempt to wrench from the hand of the Spirit his own "sword," by the perversion or abuse of which they all the more effectually slay the souls of men. It is not for us to say one word about their motives. For these they are responsible to God, and God alone can see their hearts. Let God be the judge of their motives. We say not that the men MEAN to destroy souls by perverting the Word of God, and wresting Scripture itself in support of their blasphemy. We speak not of what they intend to do, but of what they persist in doing. And we affirm, that they not only charge home upon a holy God all the iniquity which takes place among devils and men, but they wrest the very Scripture, and pervert its blessed truths in order to gain currency for their false philosophy, whereby God is dishonoured, and merchandise is made of the souls of men. In order to prove that God has foreordained all iniquity, the author of "Truth and Error" singles out the most awful crime upon record, and fathers it directly upon God's decree, and refers to the Bible itself in support of his theory. "Everything in this world [says Mr. Bonar] happens according to God's eternal arrangements. Nothing takes place except what God causes to be, or permits to be; and whatever happens in time, is decreed from eternity. EVEN THE WICKED DEED of those who crucified the Lord of Glory is said, by the apostle, to be determined before by the hand and counsel of God. Acts iv. 27, 28; also ii. 23."—*Truth and Error*, p. 37.

Here, then, is a very plain and distinct statement, on the part of our Free Church writer, and if this statement be true, we must admit that God is the author of all iniquity. But we are prepared most emphatically to deny the statement which this writer has made.

The passages of Scripture referred to DO NOT ascribe to God "THE WICKED DEED" of those who crucified the Lord of Glory. God determined beforehand to do whatever HE HIMSELF DID in the transactions of Calvary, but he never decreed any part of the wickedness which was perpetrated there, or which has been perpetrated elsewhere by devils or by wicked men. But as this assertion commits us to a full examination of the two Scripture passages which have been perverted in the quotations we have just read, we reserve such examination as the subject of our next discourse.

LECTURE FOURTH.

PRECEDENCY OF GOD'S WILL TO MAN'S WILL—"WHATSOEVER COMES TO PASS" NOT FOREORDAINED—GOD HAS NOT DECREED WICKEDNESS—MAN ALONE RESPONSIBLE FOR HIS SOUL'S SALVATION.

JAMES i. 13.—"Let no man say, when he is tempted, I am tempted of God: for God cannot be tempted with evil, neither tempteth he any man."

ACTS ii. 23.—"Him, being delivered by the determinate counsel and foreknowledge of God, ye have taken, and by wicked hands have crucified and slain."

ACTS iv. 27.—"Of a truth against thy holy child Jesus, whom thou hast anointed, both Herod and Pontius Pilate, with the Gentiles, and the people of Israel, were gathered together, for to do whatsoever thy hand and thy counsel determined before to be done."

JOHN x. 18.—"No man taketh it [my life] from me, but I lay it down of myself: I have power to lay it down, and I have power to take it again."

"NOTHING in the universe [says Mr. Bonar, in the extracts quoted in our last Lecture] takes place without the will of God. This is admitted. But it is asked, Is this will FIRST IN EVERYTHING? I answer, Yes. The will of God goes before all other wills. It does not depend on them, but they depend on it. Its movements regulate them. The 'I will' of Jehovah is that which sets in motion EVERYTHING in heaven and in earth. The 'I will' of Jehovah is the SPRING AND ORIGIN OF ALL THAT IS DONE throughout the universe, great or small, among things animate and inanimate. EVERYTHING in this world happens according to God's eternal arrangements. Nothing takes place except what God causes to be or permits to be; and whatever happens in time is decreed from eternity. EVEN THE WICKED DEED of those who crucified the Lord of Glory is said, by the apostle, to be determined before by the hand and counsel of God."

It will be observed, therefore, what the great question before us really is:—"Is the will of God FIRST IN EVERYTHING." That is the real question, we might almost say the ONLY question, to be disposed of. It is necessary that this point should be well understood and steadily kept in view. This is necessary, because the writer from whom we have now again quoted, in common with all his brethren, is constantly forgetting the question under discussion, and very generally writes and speaks and acts as if the real question were—"Is the will of God first in ANYTHING." These divines are ever and anon engaged in directing their anathemas against us, as if we denied the precedency of the Divine will in the conversion and ultimate salvation of the sinner. It is, therefore, necessary for you to understand distinctly that there is no question upon this point between us and the brethren whose doctrine we oppose. That the will of God is first in the salvation of every sinner who is saved—that this will goes before every other will, and is the spring or origin of all that is holy or excellent or fair or good in the wide universe—that whatever is good or happy in creation or providence is to be traced to the will of God as its ultimate origin or source—all this we rejoice to admit, and do constantly affirm, and stand prepared, from reason and from Scripture, unanswerably to demonstrate. It will be observed, therefore, that our opponents in argument only manifest the weakness of their cause, and the miserable position of their system of theology, when they indulge in slanderous and false assertions against the truth which they oppose and revile as heresy. It is vain for them to misrepresent and slander the sentiments of their opponents, by asserting, as they do, that our system makes the will of man to be supreme, and undeifies the Deity—that we make the sinner his own Saviour—that we deny the sovereignty and grace of God, and reduce all things to mere chance work. Such assertions as these may indeed deceive the ignorant, and impose upon indolent or prejudiced minds, who will not take the trouble to inquire for themselves; but as the progress of inquiry goes forward, and men begin to THINK and to investigate, such assertions as these will be detected in their true character, and will only expose the falsehood and the delusiveness of that system of theology which NEEDS such crutches in order to prevent its instant prostration. We have once more given prominence to the statements of a Free Church minister, in order to set the question in its true and proper position. We take it as Mr. Bonar has correctly enough stated it. It is not whether the will of God be first in ANYTHING, but, "Is this will first in EVERYTHING?" To this question the theology we oppose answers, "Yes;" while we affirm that the Word of God, and common sense itself, answers, "No." God's will is NOT first in everything; it is NOT the spring and origin of wickedness. We affirm that all that is good and excellent and blessed has been originated by God. We affirm that God's will has already set in motion the entire mechanism of redemption, and has already prepared all things necessary for the present and everlasting happiness of sinners of mankind, and has already moved downwards to earth's guilty population, and finished the work of atonement for every man's sins, and has already provided the influence of the Blessed Spirit for every man's conversion, so that "ALL THINGS ARE NOW READY," and so that every sinner who voluntarily accepts of the provision thus graciously made, is justified and sanctified and saved solely and exclusively as the result of God's will taking the precedency of his will, and bringing to his very door a free and unmerited salvation. But we do not affirm, with Mr. Bonar, that the will of God takes the precedency of the wills of devils and of men in the introduction of sin and misery into the universe. The origin of evil is not left by this writer, or by his system of theology, as anything mysterious. It is by him accounted for most fully! It is by him traced back directly to God himself! And every word, therefore, which is uttered from the pulpit, and every sentence that is emitted from the press, by Calvinistic divines, which does not father all iniquity upon a holy God, is neither more nor less nor else than a denial and condemnation of their own unscriptural and false theology—

a theology whose days are numbered, and which ought, long ere now, to have been for ever exploded.

The question, therefore, is, Whether the will of God takes the precedency of created wills in EVERYTHING? and more particularly, Whether the apostle inculcates this doctrine in the Acts of the Apostles, by ascribing even THE WICKEDNESS of those who crucified the Lord of Glory to God's unalterable decree? This is the question which presents itself for our consideration this evening. In reply to the question, we solicit your patient attention to three observations.

1. We submit, *in the first place*, that the apostle, in the passage referred to, ascribes to THE FOREKNOWLEDGE of God what has been improperly traced by Calvin and his followers to God's decree.

We have seen, in our former discourse, that the system of Calvinism does not admit the possibility of God's foreknowledge of anything which he has not himself previously decreed. It teaches men to believe that nothing which God has not himself fixed by his decree can be certain, and, as a matter of course, that nothing which is uncertain can be foreknown. According to this system, God stands in need of a decree to enlighten his mind as to the events which are hid and concealed in the womb of futurity. Short-sighted men cannot understand how anything can be foreknown as *certain*, unless the almighty will of God be previously pledged to bring it into existence. And because the proud mortal cannot understand this, he presumes, as we have formerly seen, bluntly to deny the reality, and even the possibility of it.

We humbly submit, that such a conclusion as this, is dictated by the most unreasonable vanity and pride. It is most unreasonable to deny the reality of a plainly revealed fact, simply because our limited capacities cannot apprehend the *how* and the *wherefore* of its existence. Presumption such as this, is happily no longer tolerated in our researches into the philosophy of matter, and the wonder is, that it should be tolerated and patronized, by intelligent men, when we come to investigate the philosophy of mind. And surely when we approach a theme so lofty as the philosophy of the infinite mind of the infinite Jehovah, it becomes us to lie low in the dust, and receive, like little children, the plainest statements of a well-accredited revelation. But this becoming spirit of humility seems to have been entirely cast aside by those who have hazarded the assertion, that the wickedness of our Saviour's murderers is said, by an inspired apostle, in the verses under consideration, to have been originated and decreed by God. They who discover in these verses any such statement as this, have come to the Bible with their preconceived notions, and, instead of testing their theory by the Word of God, they have interpreted the Word of God so as to suit their theory. They have come to these Scripture passages, not for the purpose of accommodating their system of theology to the Bible, but manifestly for the purpose of squaring and explaining the statements of the Bible so as to tally with their system of theology, and make the Word of God speak the language, and inculcate the most absurd and blasphemous tenets of Calvinism. Have these theologians not laid it down as an indisputable truth, that nothing can be foreseen as certain which does not happen to have been foreordained? Have they not taken it for granted, without any proof, that if anything can be said to depend on the will of man, or any created will, it is impossible even for Omniscience to apprehend its future certainty? Do they not freely speak even of GUESS WORK in connexion with omniscience, unless they are permitted to assume, and take it for granted, that everything which comes to pass has been decreed? This is what we call by the name of presumption. But it forms the source and origin of the false and erroneous interpretation, according to which "even the wicked deed of those who crucified the Lord of Glory" is said to have been "determined before by the hand and counsel of God." This is indeed the evident import of those two passages in the Acts of the Apostles, provided a man be entitled to take it for granted, that foreknowledge necessarily presupposes the existence of a foregone decree. But let this gratuitous assumption be called in question, and the verses under consideration utter no such response as that which falls upon Calvinistic ears. Deny the assumption, that whatever is foreknown must needs have been decreed, and look at the two passages of Scripture as they stand before you, and you find a very important distinction existing between the foreknowledge of God and the determinate counsel or decree of God; and then the inquiry remains, "WHAT did God

FOREKNOW?" But this does not exhaust the inquiry, for another question presents itself, and it is this—"WHAT did God DECREE in connexion with the transactions of Calvary?"

There is but *one* question, indeed, suggested by these verses, if any man may reasonably and justly confound the foreknowledge with the decree of God, and look upon them as embracing the self-same events. But if there exist an important distinction between foreknowledge and foreordination, so that anything may be certainly foreknown without having been absolutely decreed by an infinitely perfect God—if you grant the existence of such an important distinction as this, you must admit that there are *two* separate and distinct inquiries involved in the texts now under review. That such a distinction exists, is evident from the nature of the two things—the one involving no more than certain and simple apprehension, the other involving absolute and necessary causation; the one pointing to something which God knows, the other pointing to something which God causes and originates; and, as foreknowledge and decree are, in their own nature, separate and distinct, so they are distinctly and separately mentioned in the Scripture passages themselves.

What, then, did God foreknow connected with the death of his only-begotten and well-beloved Son? In reply to this question, we call your attention to two observations.

(1.) God foreknew, from eternity, with infallible

certainty, all the wickedness which was exhibited by that ungodly generation.

(2.) God foreknew, from eternity, with infallible certainty, *the possibility* of the men who acted wickedly refraining from their wickedness, and thinking and speaking and acting *otherwise* than they actually and certainly did.

He foreknew, for example, that Judas would betray Christ, and that Peter would deny him; but he also foreknew that Judas *might not* have betrayed his Master, and that Peter *might not* have denied him. But, on the supposition that the wickedness which was exhibited in connexion with the sufferings and death of Jesus had been decreed or foreordained by God, it would not be true that such wickedness was foreknown otherwise than as absolutely and necessarily certain, and so it would not be true that God could foreknow the possibility of its non-existence. To recur to the familiar examples which we have selected for the sake of illustration, it would not be true that Judas might not have betrayed Christ, or that Peter might not have denied him, if these deeds of wickedness had been unconditionally decreed. It may here be said that God might have decreed otherwise than he did decree, and so that Judas might not have betrayed and that Peter might not have denied the Saviour. But you will not fail to observe, that this assertion is made, by those who make it, for the purpose of leading our minds away from the question which now faces us. That question relates not to the decree, but to the foreknowledge of God. We inquire not, whether it was possible for God to decree otherwise than it is said he did decree; the question is, Did God foreknow the possibility of the non-existence of the wickedness of which we speak? Did he foreknow the possibility of Judas not betraying, and of Peter confessing instead of denying his Lord? To this question, Calvinism has a ready answer. "He did not foreknow any such possibility." This reply is quite consistent with the theory. It springs necessarily out of the theory. The theory is that the decree is the foundation of the foreknowledge, so that God foreknows a thing because he has decreed it. But we are told that God decreed the wickedness —he fixed, by his decree, that Judas and Peter would certainly act precisely as they did act. But it was not possible for the decree of God to fail, therefore it was not possible for Judas not to betray or for Peter not to deny the Saviour. And if it was not possible for Judas and Peter to act otherwise than they did act, God could not, of course, foreknow it to be possible.

When it is asserted, therefore, that both Judas and Peter might have acted differently, if God had been pleased to decree differently, you will see at once that this is saying nothing to the purpose. This is merely asserting the free agency of God for the purpose of evading the blunt and unequivocal denial of the free agency of man. We beg leave to hold our friends sternly to the point. When a man sins, they say truly that the man is verily blameworthy, because it was possible for him to have acted differently. We want no more of them than this good confession, and we merely insist upon their standing honestly by the obvious meaning of the words. They avow that it was possible for the man to have abstained from sinning. We press the question. What do these theologians *mean* when they avow the existence of such a possibility? Mark well, my friends, what is the reply which this theology affords to this plain and simple question: "It was quite possible for the man to have refrained from sin, because it is quite conceivable that *God, if he had so chosen, might not have decreed that the man should commit iniquity*"!! What is this but asserting the free agency of God, and at the same time denying the free agency of man? But the question *is not* whether *God* be a free agent;—the question relates to the free agency of men. The question is, "Is it possible for *men* to act differently than they do act when they choose to act wickedly?" And surely it is only a crafty and cowardly and dishonest *evasion* of this question to inform us, that "it was possible for God to have decreed differently"! Do we speak uncharitably, or do we speak honestly, when we say that this theology is a deception, and that its doctors and expounders practise a deception upon the minds and consciences of the people who follow in their wake? Speak they not daily as if they believed that man is a free and responsible agent? And, in saying this, do they not speak truly? But, under the guise of truth, do they not conceal a palpable falsehood? What is their *meaning?* They mean to say what their theology inculcates. They mean to assert the necessary dependence of man's will upon God's will "*in everything, great or small,*" in this wicked world. They say to the sinner, that he might have refrained from sin, and that he ought to have refrained from it, but their *meaning* is, that, according to God's eternal arrangements, it was not possible for the man to have acted differently!

When we, therefore, propose the question, "*What* did God *foreknow* in accordance with the statement embodied in the Acts of the Apostles?" our friends inform us that God foreknew what he himself decreed; but they tell us farther, that God decreed the wickedness. He could not, therefore, decree *the possibility* of the non-existence of the wickedness. He could not decree it to be quite possible that his own decree should fail. Surely not. Seeing, therefore, that God foreknew neither more nor less nor else than what he himself decreed, it follows that God, according to this theology, did not and could not possibly foreknow *the possibility* of the wicked men, who wickedly persecuted and blasphemed and crucified the Lord of Glory, acting differently in one single point, or refraining from one single act of sin. To recur, again, to our illustrations, God decreed that Judas and Peter should act as they did act, and he foreknew that they should so act, through the medium of his decree (which is said to be the foundation of his foreknowledge), and he did not and could not foreknow that Judas or Peter *might have acted differently*, for differently it was not possible for either of them to act without frustrating God's decree.

Our appeal is now made to a host of witnesses. We appeal to every man, woman, and child on the face of the earth, not excluding our opponents themselves. We appeal confidently to every man's own *consciousness*. We ask every man to say, whether he is not conscious within himself that, when he sins, *he might have refrained* from sinning. Is it not upon this assumption that *laws* are framed? Does not the very existence of all law, human as well as divine, proceed upon the assumption, that it is quite possible for the subjects to obey them? And do not the pains and penalties appended to the transgression of every law, assume the existence of the possibility of the transgressor acting differently? Is it not every man's duty to obey a just and righteous administration, just because it is quite possible for him to obey it?—and is it not for this very reason that the transgression of a just law is justly punishable?

Let the false philosophy which has been engrafted by Calvin upon the Word of God become dominant in society, and where are the safeguards of peace and good order and morality and liberty herself! They are overthrown and demolished by the rude hand of revolutionary ignorance. And who are the men who have trampled upon all law, human and divine, and waded through seas of blood to attain their revolutionary purposes? They have been those who have cast aside the Bible, and had their minds poisoned and their consciences seared by the philosophy of Calvin. What is *Socialism* but Calvinism without a Bible? And what is Calvinism? What is it which characterizes this system and marks it out as a theology different from the system which we seek to advance? The Free Church minister, from whom we have quoted, has himself stated the question between this theology and the system which opposes it, by asking, "Is God's will first in *everything?*"

But against this system of error we have our appeal. We have our appeal, as we have said, to the unsophisticated consciousness of universal humanity. The most hardened criminal carries along with him to the jail and to the scaffold the consciousness of blameworthiness, and this consciousness is based upon the innate conviction of the fact that HE MIGHT HAVE acted otherwise, and that it was quite POSSIBLE to have refrained from committing the crimes which have hurried him to an ignominious end. And does not the whole Bible, from beginning to end, proceed upon the principle for which we now contend? Does not every command and promise and threatening and blessed invitation of the Word of God proceed upon the great principle which universal consciousness attests, and demonstrate the truthfulness of our position, when we now maintain that every man who acts wickedly MIGHT act in consistency with conscience and the will of God?

It is, therefore, a question which affects every man's interest for time as well as for eternity. Are you disposed, my friends, to be juggled out of all that is dear to you in time, and precious throughout eternity, by this false and juggling theology? See ye not to what an awful conclusion it conducts you? Perceive ye not the false philosophy on which this system of error is avowedly based? It is based upon the denial of the freedom of man's will, save in the sense that the will of man is necessarily dependent upon and regulated by the antecedent will of God *"in everything."* It informs a wicked and godless generation, as they pursue their downward course to hell, that "everything in this world happens according to God's eternal arrangements. Nothing takes place except what God causes to be, or permits to be, and whatever happens in time, is decreed from eternity. Even the wicked deed of those who crucified the Lord of Glory is said by the apostle to be determined before by the hand and counsel of God" ! !

But we confidently submit that the Apostle says no such thing. And it is, perhaps, necessary that we should in this connexion call your attention to the apparent discrepancy between the two passages in the Acts of the Apostles, on which this assertion is avowedly based. There is no obscurity hanging over the verse which is quoted from the *second* chapter of the Acts. That verse plainly refers to the foreknowledge, as separate and distinct from the decree of God. But the verse quoted from the *fourth* chapter refers not to foreknowledge at all, and is said to trace every wickedness to "the hand and the counsel of God." I need not inform you, however, that *the translation* of that verse is not inspired—that is to say, the Calvinists who translated the New Testament Greek into the English language, laid no claim to infallibility, even in their translation. The Greek Testament is as patent and open to us as it was to the translators. We therefore state what no man can truthfully deny, when we here affirm that the verse quoted from the *fourth* chapter of the Acts is susceptible of a very different rendering, by a very simple and legitimate transposition of the words. We read it as we apprehend it ought to have been translated, when we read as follows:—"Of a truth, against thy holy child Jesus, whom thou hast anointed *for to do whatsoever thy hand and thy counsel determined before to be done*, both Herod and Pontius Pilate, with the Gentiles and the people of Israel, were gathered together." The verse, as thus rendered, does not ascribe to God's decree all that wicked men did, or any wicked thing that was done. It does not ascribe the execution of God's decree to men, but to the "holy child Jesus." He it was who was anointed for the express purpose of working out whatsoever the hand and counsel of God had determined before to be done. But should any of you prefer the translation as it stands, we submit that it does not affirm what Mr. Bonar says it affirms, even as it is read in our received translation. It does not say that God decreed "*everything*" which our Saviour's murderers chose to do, but it says that those wicked murderers were actually made instrumental in carrying into effect God's designs. They did not frustrate the great and gracious design of God in one single point, but even their *undecreed* wickedness was made subservient, not only to the *frustration* of what they wickedly hoped to effect, but even to the development of God's most wise and holy purposes. This we shall have occasion afterwards to remark upon more fully. In the mean time we have said enough to make good our position. We have endeavoured to convince you that the wickedness was not decreed, but simply foreknown. And that this wickedness was foreknown, not in the sense in which alone Calvinists admit anything to be foreknown,—not in the sense of having been absolutely and unconditionally decreed, and therefore foreknown. It was *foreknown* as *undecreed* and unoriginated and uncaused by a holy God. It was foreknown not only as certain, but as the certain result of free and responsible agents, who were not bound by any foregone decree to enact their wickedness, but who might have refrained their hands from wickedness, and their mouths from speaking guile. Herein, therefore, consists the error of this Free Church interpretation. This interpretation takes for granted what is not merely *un*proved, but what is actually *dis*proved by every man's consciousness. It takes for granted that wickedness has been decreed by God, and therefore that its existence is necessary, so that it was not possible that it might not have been committed. And taking this for granted, this false system leads its abettors to pervert the Word of God, by ascribing to his wise and holy decree what the apostle, in the passages referred to, ascribes to his foreknowledge, and his foreknowledge alone.

We need only further to remind you now, that *fore*-knowledge, like *after*knowledge, does not *cause* the existence of the object apprehended by the mind. It apprehends the certainty of the object, but it does not originate the certainty. You perceive the absurdity of imagining that your knowledge of the existence of the flood, or of the destruction of the cities of the plain, or of any other ascertained event which might be taken as a specimen, could possibly exercise any influence in bringing these events into existence. From the very nature of the case, whatever is the object of knowledge, becomes known because it is certain. It is not rendered certain because it is known. You do not say, "I know it, and therefore it exists." You rather say, "It exists, and therefore I know it." But if you had the power and the will to bring anything into existence, and forthwith were to decree it—on this supposition you would say, "I decreed it, and therefore it came to pass." In this case, your decree would be the cause of its existence. It is evident, therefore, that whatever is known is no less certain than if it were decreed. But it is plain, for this very reason, that a thing does *not need* to be decreed in order to be certain. And if a thing may be certain without being decreed, the simple question remains—"Was it not possible for *the divine mind to apprehend beforehand* the free and independent and undecreed volitions of all his intelligent and responsible creatures?"

There exists an important distinction between human

actions simply foreknown, and the same actions apprehended after they have come to pass, which will, perhaps, serve to illustrate and confirm the position in support of which we have been arguing. The wickedness which is already past is apprehended, not merely as certain, *but as something whose existence is now unavoidable, and, in that sense, necessary.* But every past sin is known by the sinner himself to have been *undecreed,* because the sinner says *truly* in reference to his sin, *"I might have avoided it."* This is attested by every man's consciousness. He knows that he has sinned, but he knows too that he might have resisted the temptation whereby he was seduced. The sins, however, which are past and gone, possess a positive necessary being. It is not possible for Omnipotence itself to blot out the fact of their actual and ascertained existence. They are in this sense necessary or unavoidable, inasmuch as after they are committed, they cannot possibly be recalled. But it is not more easy for you to certify this fact, than it is to certify the other fact to which we have adverted—the fact that such sins might have been avoided. If the sinner could only know assuredly that he was necessarily and unavoidably impelled forward to the commission of sin, he could not possibly be the subject of remorse. Would not such a plea, if well substantiated, relieve him also from punishment? But what forms the gall and bitterness of the sinner's reflection upon his folly, is the consciousness that he might have acted otherwise. Will any sophistry erase from any man's mind the consciousness of the truth which I now state? It is impossible. Here, then, is certainty—infallible certainty; no "*mere guesswork*," but absolute certainty—certainty converted into a positive necessity, by the actual existence of the object which is known. But here is something which might have been avoided, and which, therefore, was not necessary before it came into existence. It could not, therefore, be absolutely or unconditionally and eternally necessary; it could not be unconditionally and eternally decreed or foreordained.

If, then, we speak of the actions of free and responsible agents before they come into actual existence, we must say of them that they *may not* come to pass, or, in other words, that their future existence is not necessary or unavoidable. But when we say this, we do not contradict the fact of their future certainty. They are certain, whether we suppose them to be known as past, or whether we foreknow them as future. The question which, on either supposition, remains to be solved, is—*What is the cause* or foundation of their certainty? Is this cause to be discovered in the decree of God, or is it to be sought for in man's free agency? This is the sole question which presents itself for solution; for there is no doubt about the certainty of whatever is apprehended or known, whether the objects known are past or future. If, then, the decree of God is the cause or foundation of the certainty, it is evident, that the objects apprehended beforehand as certain, *must* come to pass. They cannot possibly be avoided, for it will not be imagined that the decree of God can possibly fail. But sinful actions (of which we speak) are admitted to be among those things which might have been avoided, even when they are contemplated as now and for ever necessary in point of actual existence—*i. e.*, when contemplated as past and gone. If, then, they might have been avoided, they could not possibly be decreed by God. Their cause or origin must, therefore, be traced to the perverted and abused free agency of men, seeing that it cannot be traced to the decree of God, in which case their existence would from eternity have been necessary or unavoidable. It follows, therefore, that the foreknown volitions and actions of free agents are in no sense necessary or unavoidable, but that they may or may not take place, although they be from eternity apprehended as certain.

You will observe from what has been now advanced, that strong and incontrovertible evidence of our present position lies within yourselves. You have the same evidence in support of what we have stated to you, which you have for your own existence; and it is just as easy for any man to convince himself that he does not exist, as it is to argue himself into the notion, that when he determines to walk in one direction, he cannot possibly determine to move in a different course. The consciousness of his own existence, which every man possesses, is one infallible witness to which now we make our appeal. And unless a man can honestly say, that whenever he sins against the dictates of conscience, he has only yielded to the force of a necessity which he could not possibly resist, we have that man's verdict decidedly in favour of what we now advance. The whole question resolves itself into this single point—"Was it not in my power to have determined differently?—Is there not something within me whose testimony no sophistry can contradict, which assures me that I might, and that I ought to have decided in a direction the very opposite?" When any man repents of his evil deeds, or even when he does not repent, but merely experiences internal remorse on account of his waywardness, does not that man confirm and substantiate, beyond the possibility of doubt, every statement which we make against the theory which falsely ascribes "*everything*" to God's unalterable decree?

The entire Bible confirms and strengthens the testimony of universal consciousness. Men are there addressed and treated, throughout, as possessed of that entire freedom of will, the existence of which is denied by the theology now under review. They are commanded both to will and to do in a manner the very reverse of that which they generally, we might say, universally, choose to act. And all this clearly implies the possibility of men both determining and acting in a manner very differently, and pursuing a course the very opposite of that which is too generally followed. In reference to the future, the Word of God informs men that *they may* determine on a different course from that which is certainly foreknown, and we are thereby furnished with infallible proof to convince us that wickedness which is certainly foreknown, *may not*, after all, take place, but may be avoided, and is therefore undecreed of God. If it were decreed, it must of necessity happen, and the simple question is, whether the entire volume of revelation does not confirm the testimony of every man's consciousness, and exhibit the fact that men may not, and therefore should not, act wickedly. In reference to the past, the infallible Word bears the same infallible testimony. It condemns the sinful deeds of men, and its testimony finds an honest response in the sinner's bosom, when he is assured that he might and should have willed and acted, consistently with the will of God.

But all such incontrovertible evidence is treated with contempt by the Calvinistic theology. This theology introduces a false and unscriptural *theory* among the soul-saving and soul-sanctifying truths of Scripture. It is *taken for granted* that "the will of God is first in *everything*, and that by God's immutable decree *everything* has been, from eternity, unchangeably and unconditionally fixed." And this false theory being assumed, and forced into unnatural connexion with the Word of God, the plainest truths in all the Bible are racked and tortured and mangled and destroyed, in order to make room for this monstrous and infernal conception of depraved imaginations. It is by elevating this hideous theory into the position of a first principle in theology, and twisting and perverting such texts as those now under consideration, so as to *make* them correspond exactly with this false principle, that our Free Church expositor falls into mistake, and blunders so egregiously, as to assert, that "even the wicked deed of those who crucified the Lord of Glory is said, by the apostle, to have been determined before by the hand and counsel of God." We hope we have said enough to convince you, that the wickedness referred to was not decreed, but was simply foreknown by God, and that foreknowledge embraced no antecedent decree, whereby the wickedness which comes to pass was unconditionally and divinely "*fixed;*" but, on the contrary, that the divine foreknowledge embraced the fact that this, and every other act of wickedness which disfigures the handiwork of God, it was, and is, and ever shall be, *quite possible* to avoid, up to the very moment when sin was, is, or shall be, brought into actual existence, by the undecreed and independent volitions of fallible and sinning creatures.

II. Our *second* general observation is, that in the interpretation of the verses now under consideration, the followers of Calvin ascribe to the wickedness of men, what the apostle of Christ traces directly to God's decree.

It is a remarkable fact that, like the Pharisees of old, our Free Church expositor and his friends turn the Bible upside down by their Calvinian traditions. They ascribe to God's decree what the Bible ascribes to the wickedness of men and devils, and they ascribe to the wickedness of men and devils what the Bible traces to God's unalterable and most holy decree. They thereby turn the entire Word of God upside down, and reduce its most blessed contents to one mass of inextricable confusion, and make it utter the most absurd and palpable contradictions. We have seen that those theologians ascribe all the wickedness of our Saviour's murderers to the decree of God, and we now remark, that they falsely ascribe the entire execution of God's decree to the wickedness of the men who reviled and persecuted and condemned and crucified the Lord of Glory. We say *falsely*, because it seems evident, from the word of God, that whatever God himself decreed, he himself carried into execution. What, then, did God decree? He decreed that Jesus should be, by himself, voluntarily delivered up into the hands of his enemies—that the wickedness of men should be signally defeated and frustrated, and that the men themselves should be made subservient to the working out of his most wise and holy and merciful designs.

The question suggested by this observation is very simple—Did these murderers obtain possession of the person of Jesus Christ by their own power, or did they not? Was the act whereby he was led bound to Pilate's judgment-seat the act of men, or was it the act of God? Such is the question now before us. The question is not whether the wickedness which prompted the men to seek the Saviour's life was the act of God; the question is, whether the actual *delivering up* of Christ, as a prisoner, into their hands was the result of all this wickedness, or whether it was not the direct result of God's immutable decree. In order to help you to an answer, we may refer you to the first six verses of the eighteenth chapter of John's Gospel, where we are informed that—

"When Jesus had spoken these words, he went forth with his disciples over the brook Cedron, where was a garden, into which he entered, and his disciples. And Judas also, which betrayed him, knew the place; for Jesus oft-times resorted thither with his disciples. Judas then, having received a band of men and officers from the chief priests and Pharisees, cometh thither with lanterns, and torches, and weapons. Jesus therefore, knowing all things that should come upon him, went forth, and said unto them, Whom seek ye? They answered him, Jesus of Nazareth. Jesus saith unto them, I am he. And Judas also, which betrayed him, stood with them. As soon then as he had said unto them, I am he, they went backward, and fell to the ground."

Here, then, is the most distinct answer to the question which I have now proposed. There was here a direct and miraculous interposition of Divine power, not to destroy the men, but to demonstrate to the universe the utter and the total powerlessness of all their wicked and malicious schemes. They had no power whatever to touch a hair of the Saviour's head. God could not, by an act of omnipotence, destroy their malice, or pluck out from their souls the rooted wickedness which was there. This, by an act of omnipotence,

God could not do, but he could destroy their power to hurt, by laying them prostrate on the earth. And this he, for an instant, actually did, and he thereby proved that it was not their wickedness which triumphed over him, but his matchless love which triumphed over all their malice, and which prompted him voluntarily to deliver himself into their hands, in order that he might die a ransom for their sins. In the delivering up of the Son of God into the hands of his enemies, we do not therefore behold the result or even the forth-putting of human power, but we see the direct and voluntary act of God himself in the carrying into execution his own decree. True, indeed, the wickedness of the men was not arrested in its outrageous manifestation—true, indeed, their wickedness *seemed* to triumph—but the question is, Did it triumph? So far from this, the humanity was for a moment eclipsed amid the splendour of the divinity, and God himself appeared, before the eyes of angels, of devils, and of men, to do what the whole of them together had no power to carry into execution. And what was this, but voluntarily and directly himself to execute, by his own act of holy love, what he had from eternity purposed to do, when he purposed to give his Son a ransom for all? It was not the act of the men, for "they went backward and fell to the ground." Here we behold the sole and exclusive act of God, when instantly, instead of being struck down into perdition, the men were enabled again to stand upon their feet, and received Christ a voluntary captive into their hands. Such, then, was emphatically the act of God himself, in the execution of his own decree.

And so, when Jesus was before the judgment-seat of Pilate, what did he say? "Thou couldst have no power at all against me, except it were given thee from above." Thus again did Jesus enforce the principle, that he was delivered up, and went as a lamb to the slaughter, not in consequence of the rage and malice of devils and wicked men, but as the direct and exclusive result of his Father's immutable and eternal decree. "No man [said he] taketh my life from me. I lay it down of myself. I have power to lay it down, and I have power to take it up again."

Then, indeed, did "the heathen rage, and the people imagine a vain thing." What did they vainly imagine? They imagined that they were possessed of power enough to carry into execution their own diabolical purposes against the incarnate Son of God. They gathered themselves together in order to accomplish their own wicked ends, but all in vain. "He that sits in heaven" laughed them to scorn. The Lord did hold them in derision. See Psalm ii. He proved the utter impotence of all their rage—the total powerlessness of all their mighty and apparently formidable combinations; and this he did, even at the very moment when they seemed to triumph over him and his Anointed. On the one side, there were the devil and his angels—Judas and the Jewish people—Pilate and Herod and the Roman legions—and on what were they bent?

They were bent upon the destruction of Jesus. They were leagued together in order to frustrate and overthrow the decree of God, the purport of which decree was, that his own Son should offer himself up a voluntary sacrifice, and lay down his life—not as a felon who is condemned to die—but as a conqueror, voluntarily flinging himself into the hottest of the strife, and breathing his last amid the shouts of victory,—a conqueror who, after entering into the dark abodes of death for a season, should grapple with the grim king of terrors himself, within his grim domain, and on the morning of the third day emerge triumphant from amid the gloom, crowned with the laurels of success,—a conqueror who should eventually ascend upwards, to take possession of the mediatorial throne, and wear the crown, and wield the sceptre, for evermore!

Such was the decree of God. This was what "the hand and counsel of God determined before to be done." But Herod and Pontius Pilate, with the Gentiles and the people of Israel, had no such ends or purposes in contemplation. The very reverse of all this was their unholy and malignant intent. But they were defeated—manifestly defeated—inasmuch as, *in the first place*, God did, in point of fact, himself accomplish what he decreed from eternity to do. This God himself did, in spite of all the rage of his enemies against him and his Anointed One. And, *in the second place*, God executed his own decree, and did his own work, in such a way—at such a time—and amid such a combination of circumstances, that it really seemed as if his enemies had been intentionally gathered together to do his work, which work they unwittingly and unintentionally forwarded and advanced. And thus it was that, at that very moment when they were raging and foaming and battling against him, they were made instrumental in forwarding and advancing "whatsoever the hand and counsel of God determined before to be done."

But it was not *the wickedness* of those who crucified the Lord of Glory, whereby the eternal purpose of God was fulfilled even unintentionally on the part of those ungodly men. The wickedness was never decreed by God, and even in the hour of its apparent triumph, whatever was wicked and unholy, was most effectually and gloriously frustrated and overthrown. All that was sinful and malicious was traceable to the willing and the doing—the designing and the determining of the men, and all this was triumphantly defeated, even when it seemed to have effected its designs. All that was good and gracious, was but the development in time, of God's decree formed from eternity, and all this was most gloriously accomplished by God himself; so that while their wickedness was defeated, the very men who were fighting against God with all their might, were made subservient to the execution of his purposes.

We have already hinted, that the verse which is erroneously supposed to father the wickedness of our Saviour's persecutors on the decree of God, and to teach that such wickedness was the actual fulfilment of that decree, is susceptible of a very different interpretation, by a legitimate alteration in the collocation of the words. But we intimated, at the same time, that even as the verse stands in the received translation, it does not inculcate the doctrine which has been erroneously founded upon it.* This will appear evident from

* On Acts iv. 27, 28, Dr. Payne observes—"This is a case, as it is said, in which sinful actions are spoken of as the consequence of a Divine decree. Now, I do not avail myself of a different collocation of the words, proposed by some eminent scholars, which bring out the statement, not that Herod and Pontius Pilate, &c., were gathered together to do what the counsel of the Lord had determined, but that Christ was anointed to accomplish all this. I do not avail myself of this, both because it is unnecessary to resort to this altered collocation of the words, and because there can be no doubt that the salvation of men, by the crucifixion of the Son of God, was a Divinely appointed event. . . . . . In this case, the Divine decree extended to the giving up of the Saviour into the hands of his enemies, but not to the treatment which, when thus given up, he received from them. Known unto God are all his works, and all the power, the thoughts, the feelings of men, from eternity. He knew the precise state of mind of Herod and Pontius Pilate, &c. . . . . . . And yet, knowing all this, he *sent* his Son into the world; he *determined* to send him into the world—*determined* to surrender him to the malice of his enemies. . . . . . . Though HE DID NOT DECREE that Herod and Pontius Pilate, &c., should bind and bruise and crucify the Saviour, he did decree that the Saviour should be given up to their cruelty and vengeance. His decree, in short, extended to what he did in this transaction, but NOT TO WHAT MEN DID. . . . . . . Jehovah perceives how that principle, which is the prolific source of all evil, will develop itself in every conceivable variety of circumstances. And it is perfectly easy for him so to arrange his providential dispensations, as that the ungodly passions of men shall prove

the observations which have latterly been submitted for your consideration. It seems quite evident that Herod and Pontius Pilate and the Gentiles did most unintentionally do what God intended to be done. But in doing this, they did the very reverse of what they had wickedly determined. Their wicked designs were the very opposite of what God did not only decree, but carry into execution, in actual opposition to the determinations of wicked men. Granting, therefore, that the common rendering ought rather to be preferred, the verse which says to us that those wicked men did whatever *God* purposed, assures us by that very statement, that *God did not* decree any portion of their wickedness, seeing that such wickedness was frustrated and overthrown.

So far, then, from informing us that "God foreordained whatsoever comes to pass," or hinting that "the will of God is first in *everything*," or announcing that "even the wicked deed of those who crucified the Lord of Glory was determined before by the hand and counsel of God,"—the inspired apostle intimates exactly the *reverse*, and that, too, in the verses which have been selected as the stronghold of Calvinism!

It is evident, therefore, from the Word of God, as

the instruments of accomplishing his merciful purposes, without decreeing that these men shall be the subjects of this depravity, or that their unholy passions shall develop themselves in that particular manner; or, I add, without DECREEING TO PERMIT either the one or the other. All that God does in the business, is the subject of decree; all that man does is not the subject of decree."—*Lecture VII., on Sovereignty*, pp. 125–127.

well as from the nature of the case, that the system of theology which is based upon an assumption such as that under examination, stands upon a sandy foundation. The storm of controversy which has happily begun to beat against the baseless tenement, and the tide of discussion which has already begun to rise upwards around its walls, must very speedily insure its downfall. It is not founded upon the Rock of Ages, and the sooner it is laid prostrate on the earth, and swept away for ever, so much the better for the interests of truth and the well-being of immortal souls.

III. We submit, in the third place, that the interpretation which has been given of these two verses in the Acts, by the supporters of Calvinism, CANNOT POSSIBLY be correct.

There are some statements which are so evidently inconsistent with truth, that every honest man is able to detect their falsehood the moment they are uttered. It needs little or no examination in order to pronounce them to be false and unfounded. And so there are some interpretations of the Word of God which are so manifestly inconsistent with the whole tenor and import of Scripture declaration, that every man who is in the slightest degree acquainted with his Bible, feels constrained, at the very first glance, to reject them and trample them under his feet, as perversions of the Word of God. As if the atheist should say to you that it is written in the first verse of the fourteenth psalm, that "there is no God"—appealing to the very Bible, which in such an event would be divested of all authority—in proof of his blasphemous assertion. On such a supposition as this, your reply would be instantaneous and unhesitating—"The fool hath said in his heart, there is no God;" but that there is a God all Nature speaks aloud through all her works, and to the voice of universal Nature, the entire volume of Scripture adds its unanswerable response. It is plain, at first sight, that whatever is evidently opposed to the universal testimony of Scripture and of conscience, cannot possibly be true. Of this nature is the interpretation of the two passages which we are now examining. According to this, we are called upon to believe that all the wickedness which takes place among men has its origin in the heart of God, and its original embodiment in the purpose of God, and is neither more nor less than the execution in time, of what God has purposed from eternity to bring to pass. This is what we are informed the Bible declares. And when any man startles at such an announcement, just as he shrinks from the reception of the statement—there is no God, he is informed, with a grave countenance and a pious whine, that God is sovereign, and it is his duty to receive as a truth the blasphemous declaration. But most certain it is, that every man who will listen to the voice of his own conscience (not to speak of the Word of God at all), must shrink back instinctively from the assertion, that God has himself originated every abomination which we call by the name of sin, by first decreeing its existence from eternity, and then himself executing his decree in the works of creation and providence, and thus by his omnipotence bringing it to pass in time. If there be any meaning in language, what is this but to assert that God himself is the active agent in the commission of all iniquity, and that he has deliberately purposed from eternity to bring it to pass! What are men but the passive instruments in his hand, to carry into execution whatever enormity his hand and counsel hath determined to do! What are the circumstances of time and the events of Providence amid which men are placed, but the means which God uses for the one purpose of hemming up their path and constraining them to perpetrate the innumerable acts of wickedness which he hath decreed to bring to pass! This is what we are called upon to believe; and not only so, but we are gravely informed that this is precisely what the Bible teaches us. Now I most unhesitatingly affirm, that it is as easy for any man so far to stifle his conscience, as to believe that there is no God at all, as to believe that there is such a God as Calvinism has set up. I put it fearlessly to your own consciences, and I ask you to say if you do not find it impossible to believe that God is not only the originator of all evil, but at the same time the great executioner of it—himself executing certain decrees which necessitate sin, in the works of creation and providence! But here is the fearful picture which you have set up before you, and which the writer, from whom I have quoted, calls a representation of God, and which he commands you to fall down and worship. He directs you to Pilate's judgment-seat, and to the blood-thirsty rabble who crowded around it. He points you to the innocent Jesus arraigned before that judgment-seat, and cruelly and unjustly charged with crimes of which he was guiltless as a lamb. He calls upon you to mark the deliberate villany of the men who knew that their victim was innocent, but who suborned false witnesses, and brought them forward to substantiate, by what they knew to be lies, their malignant charge. And what does this writer say to you, and what does he ask you to believe? He admits that all this is very wicked, and he asks you to condemn and execrate the atrocious deed. And so far it is well. But he instantly changes the scene. The curtain which *concealed something else* from your gaze is drawn aside. And what do you see? It is the image of a Being who has been *behind the scenes*, managing and ordering and arranging the dreadful tragedy. Here is the originator of the entire plot exhibited before you. The affair was all of his planning. He it was who originally decreed, and finally executed the whole. There stands the image of the Being who suggested and manufactured the false and infamous charge. He had power and resources enough at his disposal to shut up those ruffians falsely to prefer it, and he resolved to exert his ingenuity and power to that effect. He it was who hatched and ordained the infernal falsehoods whereby that unjust charge should be substantiated, and he took care so to order all events that those false witnesses should have their consciences seared, so as to stand prepared to swear to what they knew to be a lie.

There, then, is the prime mover, and the secret executioner, of the whole behind the scenes. But what comes next before you? Who is this who seems ready to relent and set the victim of injustice free? It is Pontius Pilate himself. There is tenderness in his eye—there is compassion in his heart—there is a tremulous, hesitating sound proceeding from his lips. Ah! he seems reluctant to condemn. What is that which fell from his lips? Surely—surely the innocent is acquitted, for PILATE has said, "I find no fault in him." He thinks of the fearful dream which, but the night before, had startled from her slumbers the wife of his bosom. He looks on that majestic countenance—calm and commanding in its consciousness of innocence,—he trembles to condemn, and, under the impulse of his better nature, Pilate exclaims, "I find no fault in him."

But here, again, the scene is changed. Again the mysterious curtain is withdrawn by this modern teacher of modern Christianity. Again does this Free Church teacher point you to the Being who has decreed the whole, and who is secretly but infallibly directing the infernal plot. The heart even of Pontius Pilate relents, and fain would he set free the innocent. But this Being, whose image is held up before you, has bound down Pilate, by an iron decree, to dash the tear of pity from his eye, and stifle the sentiment of justice within his soul, and drown the voice of faithful conscience, as she urges him to let the victim go. And, in the execution of this decree, instantly, as if to drown the voice of imploring conscience, is Pontius Pilate forced to listen to ten thousand voices exclaiming, "*Crucify him, crucify him!* If thou let this man go, thou art not Cæsar's friend." It is as if the bottomless pit were opened up, and all the fiends of hell let loose upon him, in order to force him to spill the blood of the innocent; and—*there stands the originator of the whole!*—the Being who has decreed all this!—the Being who has shut up Pilate to the necessity of doing what it is most evident he would not otherwise have done! And *who is this* Being who has urged on all this wickedness? What is his name? Alas! alas! that so many should call him GOD!!! SATAN *is his proper name.*

I ask you to look at the text from the epistle of James, and see whether you have not there a very different picture of the Deity from that which is set before you by this most blasphemous interpretation of the two statements embodied in the Acts. The Holy Spirit says expressly, that God cannot so much as tempt any man to sin. But this disciple of Calvin declares that God does more than tempt—he shuts up men to the necessity of sinning, by an unalterable decree, even as his decree originated, and his omnipotence insured, the perpetration of all the wickedness of the men who shed the Saviour's blood!!

Permit me, in conclusion, earnestly and affectionately to remind every one of my hearers, that there devolves upon each one of us a solemn and a tremendous responsibility, which, in the midst of this exciting controversy, we are too prone to forget. We are, each man and woman present, responsible to God for our own personal and individual salvation. This is what Calvinism teaches us to forget. It devolves the entire responsibility upon God, and takes it away from the consciences of men; and herein it appeals to the innate depravity and spiritual slothfulness of humanity, and to this circumstance alone it owes its popularity and its success. It feeds and it fattens upon the depravity of human nature, and to this alone does it owe its existence at the present hour. There is, my dear friends, a fatal tendency in human nature universally, to roll upon God the entire responsibility of everything that happens among men. There is a tendency, in our depraved and corrupted minds, to rid themselves of the burden of personal responsibility, and to sit or recline at ease under a gospel despised, and an atonement rejected, and a Holy Spirit resisted, and a sin-laden condemned soul still unconverted, and every moment exposed to eternal woe. There is a fatal tendency in every mind to shield itself from the stings and reproaches of a faithful conscience, under the hypocritical pretence of guarding the sovereignty, and intermeddling not with the province of God. You are, it may be, yet unconverted—yet unsaved—yet without "peace with God through our Lord Jesus Christ." And when conscience, faithful to her trust, would arouse you from your slumbers; and while the Holy Spirit says to you, "Behold I stand at the door and knock;" and while God himself is even beseeching you to be reconciled;

what are you about? You are probably soothing your consciences by the hypocritical pretence of "WAITING GOD'S TIME, OR DAY OF POWER." See ye not that ye are thereby casting upon God the entire responsibility of your present unconverted—unsaved—God-dishonouring and Saviour-despising position? O my fellow-sinner, why wilt thou not open thine eye upon the great reality, and behold the God who loves your soul waiting—already waiting—compassionately waiting—WAITING FOR THEE? You do not need to wait another moment for thy God. He has waited long, and he is infinitely desirous even now for thy conversion, but we cannot say to any one among you, that he will wait another week or day or hour. "Behold, NOW is the accepted time; behold, NOW is the day of salvation." The entire responsibility of your present unsaved state rests entirely upon your own heads, and if you perish eternally, that system of error, whereby you are now deluded, will not come to your rescue in the place of woe, but you shall sink down to hell under the awful burden which now you seek in vain to shift entirely upon the decree of an Almighty God. On your own heads will rest your own soul's blood; and it will be too late to lament the day when you yielded up your souls to the influence of a false philosophy—a man-made creed—and wasted away your day of grace under the specious and hypocritical pretext of waiting upon that God who in reality is waiting for you. The man who tells you that it is not the sinner who moves first in the matter of conversion, tells you what is truth. But that man who says to you that God has not ALREADY moved forward, and has not ALREADY taken his place, and is not ALREADY propitiated and satisfied for your sins, and is not ALREADY waiting to receive you even now into the bosom of his love—that man, whoever he be, is a deceiver of your souls. THE FIRST STEP HAS ALREADY BEEN TAKEN by your God, and on yourselves alone now rests the tremendous responsibility of your soul's conversion. Ah! it will serve you nothing—if you continue determined in your present course, and rush onward to perdition—to say to your souls that you were not so presumptuous as to take the matter out of the hand of a sovereign God, nor so unorthodox in your creed as to be beforehand with God in your salvation. If you will not look at this hypocritical pretext, this cunning slander against God's truth, in the light of the gospel revelation, you will see it clearly enough exposed and burned up by the flames of hell. You will see, when it shall be too late, that it was a mere device of Calvinism, to lull your conscience asleep for time, and pander to your innate depravity, and leave you at your ease without "PEACE WITH GOD." You will see that it was a foul slander against the truth of God to insinuate, that should you venture even now to believe in Christ as your atoning sacrifice, who died for your sins, you would be beforehand with God, and become your own Saviour, and anticipate and forestal the grace of the Spirit of God, without which, no sinner can indeed be saved. You will see that God was always beforehand with you, and anticipated your every want; and sent his Son to bear the punishment of your sins, that you might not yourselves be punished, but go free; and sent the Holy Spirit to point you to the finished work of Jesus, as the glorious and exclusive ground of your sal vation. And you will see that all things being thus ready for your immediate conversion, you were yourselves responsible for doubting the truth of God, and hesitating and slumbering and perishing on the very threshold of salvation. If you will not open your eyes and look upon the delusions of a false theology now, and see it now exposed by the light of the gospel, you shall ere long see its falsehood exposed in the fires of perdition. Depend upon it, my friends, that ON YOUR OWN PRESENT CHOICE, and that alone, does your present and eternal well-being NOW depend. "All things are ready." "Choose ye this day whom ye will serve." GOD THE FATHER is willing, GOD THE SON is willing, GOD THE SPIRIT is willing. On your OWN WILL, therefore, hangs NOW your everlasting destiny. And the theology which would teach you to wait or hesitate or procrastinate, as if either the Father or the Son or the Spirit needed to be waited upon, in order to be made willing to save you, or as if all that is needful for your immediate pardon were not, on the part of God, ALREADY FINISHED, or as if the will of God had not ALREADY ANTICIPATED your will, and is not ALREADY MOVING for your rescue, —the theology which blasphemously assumes that all things ARE NOT READY for your immediate acceptance, and for the immediate acceptance of every sinner on this side of hell, and which would scare you away from salvation by the pharisaical pretence, the hypocritical whine, about the imaginary sin and danger of YOUR WILL going before, and moving heavenward, independently of THE WILL OF GOD—such a theology is the most successful instrument whereby Satan deceives and ruins precious and immortal souls. Depend upon it, that if you are still doubting, and without peace in the prospect of meeting God, the fault is ALL YOUR OWN. The cause in not with God, but with yourselves. You have the power to will this moment your own salvation. And it will be said to you, when it is too late, if you shall live and die unsaved, not that God was ever unwilling, but

"THE CHOICE YOU MADE has fixed your doom;
For this is Heaven's decree,
That with the fruits of what he sow'd
The sinner fill'd shall be."
—*Par. X., on Prov.* i. 20–31.

Already has God come down to you, and even now he waits and entreats and strives most earnestly for your salvation. THE DECISION NOW RESTS ENTIRELY WITH YOURSELVES.

LECTURE FIFTH.

THEORY SECOND, OR ELECTION TO A SPECIAL OR EXCLUSIVE INFLUENCE OF THE HOLY SPIRIT—THIS THEORY EQUALLY UNSCRIPTURAL WITH THAT FORMERLY EXAMINED—SUBVERSIVE OF THE UNITY OF THE GODHEAD.

ISAIAH v. 3, 4.—"Judge, I pray you, betwixt me and my vineyard. What could have been done more to my vineyard, that I have not done in it?"

EZEKIEL xxxiii. 11.—"As I live, saith the Lord God, I have no pleasure in the death of the wicked; but that the wicked turn from his way and live: turn ye, turn ye from your evil ways; for why will ye die, O house of Israel?"

MATTHEW xxiii. 37.—"O Jerusalem, Jerusalem, thou that killest the prophets, and stonest them which are sent unto thee, how often would I have gathered thy children together, even as a hen gathereth her chickens under her wings, and ye would not!"

WE proceed now to call your attention to the second general theory of election. The theory already examined, claims for the elect a special and exclusive interest in the death of Christ. It affirms that Jesus shed his blood upon the cross for the elect alone. The doctrine now to be examined, claims for the elect a special and exclusive interest in the work of the Spirit. It affirms that the Spirit of God exerts his influence upon the minds of the elect alone, and that the Spirit strives with none of the human race excepting the elect, with the view of bringing them to salvation. This theory has been resorted to with the view of reducing the doctrine of Calvin to a more seeming consistency with the Word of God, and of rendering its dogmas somewhat more palatable to the generality of mankind. The school of theologians by whom this doctrine has been patronized, have been sometimes distinguished by the name of "Moderate Calvinists," while they who have pled for a limitation of the atonement of Christ, as well as for a limitation of the influence of the Spirit, have been styled, "Ultra-Calvinists." The great difference between these two parties consists in this—the Moderate Calvinist affirms that Jesus died equally for all men, while the Ultra-Calvinist denies this affirmation, and contends that Jesus died for the elect only. We have, therefore, one set of Calvinists contradicting another set of Calvinists, on what is, beyond all question, the most important doctrine of Christianity—the doctrine of the atonement.

The doctrine, then, which falls now to be considered, proceeds upon the fullest admission of the great truth, that the Son of God shed his blood for every sinner of the human race. This is an admission which the greater proportion of professed Calvinists have latterly felt themselves constrained to make. The men have been latterly shut up to this conclusion by the force of truth, and the rapid advance of Scripture knowledge among the great bulk of professing Christians. There are few men who have given to the all-important inquiry the slightest investigation, without perceiving, at a glance, that since the death of Christ is the only Scriptural and consistent ground of the gospel offer, the atonement must of necessity be as extensive as the offer; and therefore, considering that the offer of pardon and salvation is made to all men, the Saviour of the world must have died for all men. The atonement is the foundation of which the gospel offer is the superstructure; and the great bulk of theologians have been compelled to admit, that the foundation must be as wide as the superstructure; so that already, in the progress of the discussion, the Ultra-Calvinists have been left in a small and humiliating minority. But while this doctrine admits the universality of the death of Christ, it still maintains the limitation of the influence of the Spirit. It has *the appearance* of greater liberality and freeness, and comes to men with a far more imposing and generous aspect, than the doctrine which we have already discussed. We shall see, however, that all this liberality and all this vaunted consistency with the universal call of the gospel to all men without exception, is more in appearance than reality, and that this half-and-half theory—this measure of a crooked and halting policy—is no less decidedly contradicted by the Word of God, than the theory which the middle men have been constrained to forsake and to condemn.

I. WE OBSERVE, IN THE FIRST PLACE, THAT THIS DOCTRINE RETAINS SOME OF THE MOST OBJECTIONABLE PRINCIPLES OF THAT UNSCRIPTURAL THEORY WHICH WE HAVE ALREADY EXAMINED.

There can be no doubt that it is a most important truth which is admitted, when it is conceded that Jesus died for all. And there is in the admission of this great truth, a clear way of escape from the unscriptural position, that God, in any case, is bound in justice to justify those sinners for whom the Saviour died. And thus far this theory is free from one fatal objection, to which, as we have seen, the former theory stands exposed.

But, while the doctrine now under consideration adopts and recognises a great and important truth, it retains and embraces a great proportion of the error with which we have already proved the former theory to be burdened. It rejects one part of the error of Calvin, but it retains another part of the same error; and while it leaves men in a position no less hopeless than that in which it found them, this theory wants the consistency of the system which it professes to supplant. It agrees with the former in tracing *whatsoever* comes to pass to the sovereign pleasure and the unalterable decree of God. It asserts, indeed, that it was the will of God to give his Son to die for all men, and in asserting this it admits a very important truth; but it asserts, at the same time, that God has, in sovereignty, decreed and purposed to withhold his Spirit from all men except the elect, and in asserting this it retains a very important error. This theory does not say that God executes his decree, and carries into effect his determination to condemn all save the elect, by giving up his Son to die for the elect, and the elect alone. It affirms that Christ died for the non-elect as well as for the elect, but that God has unconditionally decreed that the former shall not be saved, and therefore he has purposed to keep back from them the influence of the Spirit. You will notice, therefore, that this doctrine leaves men in exactly the same position in which it found them—under an absolute impossibility of being saved—unless it be true that men can indeed be saved without the influence of the Holy Spirit, and in direct opposition to the sovereign purpose and eternal decree of Jehovah.

Now my question is this—Wherein does this theory differ practically and fundamentally from that other theory which we have, in our former Lectures, proved in your hearing to be utterly opposed to the Scriptures of truth? I have already granted that it does differ, in mere theory, from that which has been already shown to be unscriptural, but the question is—Where lies the practical difference? There is, I admit, a greater sound of liberality and Scripture consistency, but my question is—Whether all this apparent and vaunted liberality does not amount to mere empty sound, and nothing more? There is a great admission, I grant you, when the doctrine, that Jesus died for all men, is no longer denied; but the question is—Whether the poison be not mingled with the wine?—whether the great doctrine of Christ's death for all men be not paralyzed and destroyed, and rendered practically useless to the souls of men, by being associated with the exhibition of a dark decree, whereby all men, except the elect, are shut out and expelled from the very possibility of tasting the benefits of the great atonement?

Permit me to read to you one short extract from an eminent living divine—a divine who has written one of the best treatises for the express purpose of establishing the great and glorious doctrine, that Jesus died for all men, without one solitary exception. "The brethren of Joseph spoke truly of themselves [says Dr. Wardlaw] when they whispered one to another, 'We are verily guilty concerning our brother, in that we saw the anguish of his soul, when he besought us, and we would not hear; therefore is this distress come upon us.' Conscience was in the right. They *were* verily guilty. And yet it was the purpose of God, by means of their unbrotherly envy and cruelty, to fulfil his prophetic declarations to Abraham respecting the future history of the nation that was to spring from his loins. It was not the less their duty to be affectionate and kind to their brother, that such affection and kindness would have disarranged and frustrated the whole counsel of God; nor was it the less their sin to violate the claims of fraternal love, that by such violation they fulfilled it."—*Discourses on the Atonement*, p. 184.

Be pleased, then, to mark well what is here said. Had the brethren of Joseph not done what was sinful, the divine decree would have been disarranged and frustrated; and in doing what was sinful, these men are said to have been acting in consequence of, and consistently with, the immutable purpose and decree of God!

Now, we have already endeavoured to prove that such a doctrine is opposed to the plainest declarations of Scripture, and cannot possibly be true. It is a libel upon the character of God, and is opposed to the common apprehensions of mankind. The writer from whom I have just quoted says, that the decree and counsel of God would be frustrated if men did not act wickedly. If the murderer did not murder his victim—if the adulterer did not indulge his licentious passion—if the drunkard did not quench his unnatural thirst—if the blasphemer did not utter his horrid blasphemy—if, in a word, all things did not happen exactly as they come to pass, the decree and purpose of God would be frustrated!! And what is this, but just to embrace the most horrible doctrine of Ultra-Calvinism? It is for the express purpose of leaving room for the free and necessary execution of such horrible decrees, that the supporters of this theory find it necessary to limit and circumscribe the Holy Spirit, in his strivings with mankind. They do not like to say that God actually exerts his power for the purpose of insuring the sin and the damnation of his creatures. To assert this would not be *very expedient!* They choose rather to present the horrid conception in a milder and more palatable form. He only keeps back his Spirit, and withdraws his grace. He sees that if his Spirit were to plead with men, they would not act wickedly. He determines, however, that the wickedness shall come to pass; and if it were not to come to pass, his purpose and decree would be frustrated. And so, in order to insure the commission of the wickedness, he has resolved, in sovereignty, to leave the men without the Spirit—without which he knows they will be sure to transgress. This is the form in which the decree of God is presented before us by the *expediency* theory of which we speak. And I now put it to your candid and unprejudiced judgments to say, if there be not here a full development of the most hideous error, I had almost said blasphemy, of the system which we have already proved to be unscriptural. If the murderer shall place his victim in a situation in which he has so arranged that the man shall necessarily die, and from which all that is necessary for the sustenance of existence is withdrawn, he is no less truly a murderer than if, with his own hand, he had plunged the dagger into his bosom. King David did not, with his own hand, murder Uriah the Hittite—he only ordered the man to be placed in the front of the battle, and the necessary assistance to be withheld from him. But the mode in which the murder was committed, did not alter the nature of the deed. And so here, when we are informed that God does not infuse sin into men's minds by a direct act of his omnipotence, but that he has decreed the wickedness, and only brings it to pass, by withholding the one only influence needful to prevent it—we do not discover any real difference between this doctrine and that other theory which has been formerly examined and condemned by the plainest statements of God's own Word.

But while there exists no real difference between this middle theory and that extreme doctrine formerly considered, I do most earnestly entreat you, my beloved friends, to compare them both with the strong and emphatic declarations embodied in the two passages of Scripture to which your attention has been directed. Does God himself not appeal to men, and ask them there what more he could do for his vineyard which he hath not done? What, then, is the reply which this theory makes to this important question? It says that God could have done far more for sinners who perish than what he has done or purposed to do. It informs us most distinctly that God could, if he had so chosen, have given to his vineyard the dews of the Divine influence, but this he has, in sovereignty, purposed to withhold. He knew well that if the influence of the Spirit had been given to his vineyard it would bring forth grapes in rich abundance. He knew well that if the influence of the Spirit was withheld and kept back from his vineyard, it would bring forth wild grapes. He purposed from eternity that it should bring forth wild grapes and thorns and briars, and every noxious weed; but to bestow the influence of the Spirit—to cause the dew to descend upon it from on high, would be most effectually to frustrate and disarrange his high counsel, and therefore we are informed he withholds the special influence. I appeal to those plain texts of Scripture, which I have read in the outset, against such an exhibition as this gives us of the character of our God. I do not deny God's right and title to keep back and withhold from men the influence of his Spirit. I do not deny that God, if he were treating us as we deserve, would never approach us more with the gentle drawings or the earnest strivings of his grace. O who can deny all this, or presume to say that we have any claim, in justice, to one single manifestation of the Holy Spirit to our souls! But all this does not render the doctrine we are now considering one shade the brighter. This admission only manifests more clearly and decidedly its dark and odious features, and brings it out more prominently in all its dreadful and hideous deformity. We can lay no claim whatever to the influence of the Holy Spirit, for God might in perfect equity most justly withhold it from us all. Let this be most readily granted, for verily this is most true; and yet the question still remains, does God condescend to treat men as they have no right to be treated as respects the influence of the Spirit—that blessed influence, without which no fruit of holiness can possibly take root and flourish within the human soul? If God does not keep back his Spirit, but if that Spirit does, in point of fact, strive with wicked and ungodly men—although we do admit that men have no claim to his influence—is it not for this very reason all the more sinful, and all the more cruel, and all the more blasphemous in the Church to deny and hide from the eyes of perishing men this most wonderful act of Sovereign Grace? The very circumstance that men do not deserve the influence of the Spirit, and that God would do them no injustice were he to withhold it, renders the enormity of the crime a thousand-fold more glaring, on the part of men, when they presume to say that this needful influence is withheld. Now, if it had been kept back from wicked men God could not have been blamed; but this we do most unhesitatingly affirm, God could not appeal to men as he does, and ask themselves to say what more it was possible for him to do for them which he hath not done, in order to bring them to repentance. This God could not, and would not say, if he did, in point of fact, withhold from them the very influence needful for their return to himself. Would it in this case be presumption in men to reply, in answer to this earnest and touching appeal, "True, O God, thou hast given thy Son to die for us, thy vineyard—true, thou hast most graciously addressed to us thy blessed gospel call—true, thou art under no obligation to thy vineyard to visit it with the dew of thy influence—but, O Lord, thou knowest that without this we cannot bring forth fruit unto thy glory, and thou canst do something more for thy vineyard which thou hast not yet done—thou canst impart the influence of the Spirit; and now, seeing that thou hast most graciously appealed to thy vineyard itself, and called upon men to say what more thou canst do that thou hast not done, grant but this one farther influence, and we shall instantly flourish and bring forth fruit, and appear fair and lovely as the garden of the Lord." I ask any man to say if this is not the precise reply which wicked men would be in a position to give to the question which our God has most graciously condescended to propose. But what is the rejoinder which the doctrine we are now considering puts into the lips of God? It makes God say that all this is very true, but nevertheless he has made a decree whereby these wicked men must necessarily and inevitably sin against him and be damned, and this decree would be frustrated and disarranged (to use the words of the writer already quoted) if the needful influence was not kept back; and therefore, while it is most true that he could do something more to his vineyard, he has determined, in sovereignty, that the one thing needful shall not be done! I now most solemnly appeal to you, men and brethren, in vindication of the injured and maligned character of our God; and I call upon you to decide in the face of God's own word, and this evening to say whether such a doctrine as this be not utterly inconsistent with its plainest, and most obvious, and most impressive announcements. I add to this appeal to his own vineyard the oath of God himself, wherein he most emphatically contradicts the doctrine which has been palmed upon his Church—"As I live, saith the Lord God, I have no pleasure in the death of the wicked; but rather that the wicked turn from his way and live. Turn ye, turn ye from your evil ways; for why will ye die, O house of Israel?"

Brethren, the question is a solemn one—and it is a question which will meet you at the judgment-seat. Will ye any longer set aside the oath of Jehovah himself, by lending your ears or your influence to perpetuate and uphold the mere traditions of fallible men?

II. I OBSERVE, IN THE SECOND PLACE, THAT THIS THEORY OF ELECTION IS STILL MORE OBJECTIONABLE

THAN THAT WHICH WE HAVE FORMERLY EXAMINED, INASMUCH AS IT INFRINGES UPON THE UNITY OF THE GODHEAD.

According to this doctrine, we are informed that God the Father so loved the whole world, without exception, as to give up his own Son to die in its stead. We are farther informed, that God the Son regarded from eternity the whole human race with an equal regard, so that He, in the fulness of the time, came, and voluntarily offered up himself the propitiation, not for the sins of the elect only, but also for the sins of the whole world. All this is most fully admitted by the brethren who adhere to, and support the theory of election now under consideration. This they have found it impossible to deny. The storm of controversy within their own church* has literally driven them to the admission of this much of the great and glorious truth. But, in place of sailing into the safe and peaceful haven which was open for their reception, they have been drifted upon the rocks and the sand-banks of error, by turning round in order to embrace the great fundamental delusion now before us. Their position is no better than it was before; nay more, it is, if possible, still worse, and must inevitably prove still more disastrous. For what does this theory involve? It involves the denial of the same mind in God the Spirit, which they are compelled to look upon as dwelling in God the Father and God the Son. The love of the Father and

* Reference is here made to the United Secession, now merged into THE UNITED PRESBYTERIAN CHURCH.

the work of the Son they now see to be universal—wide as the world—embracing in its ample bosom the entire family of man, without distinction and without exception. But their Confession of Faith informs them that God has determined to send down to destruction the greater portion of the human family, and that from all those whom he has created and brought into the world for damnation, God withholdeth his grace, and exposeth them to such objects as their corruption makes occasion of sin; and farther, gives them up to their own lusts, to the temptations of the world, and to the power of the devil—all in order to prevent the possible frustration, and the sure and certain execution of his own decree. And so, in order to preserve the credit of a man-made creed, the third person in the blessed Godhead is arrayed against the other two; and while the love of the Father and the love of the Son embraces the whole world, the love of the Holy Spirit is restricted and confined solely and exclusively to the elect! The wishes, and the desires, and the gracious efforts of the Holy Spirit, are not by any means co-extensive with the wishes, and desires, and amazing efforts of the Father and the Son for the salvation of mankind! That God the Father earnestly and sincerely desires, or wills that all men should be saved, is unanswerably argued by the upholders of this doctrine from the Word of God. They argue, with the inspired apostle, that God has proved that he wills all men to be saved, by the fact that he has given his Son a ransom for all men. They point to the death of Jesus for every sinner of the human race, and they do most triumphantly conclude therefrom, that God the Father and God the Son do most earnestly and sincerely desire every sinner on the face of the earth to be saved. But when they come to the work of the Holy Spirit they say, that this great work is limited and circumscribed. And just as from the work of the Son they argue out the desire, the earnest desire of God, that all for whom his Son was given to die should believe and live, even so are we taught to measure the desire and the wish of the Spirit. The Spirit, accordingly, does not wish all men to be saved! The Spirit's work and effort is the measure of his love. And since his work and his effort to save does not extend beyond the number of the elect, we have the Holy Spirit represented as not willing that any one single soul, beyond the number of the elect, should come to the knowledge of the truth and be saved from impending ruin.

Here, then, is the desire and the wish of both the Father and the Son opposed and counteracted by the desire of the Spirit! Here is the Father parting with his only-begotten and well-beloved Son, just because he desires to save a world from perdition; and here is the Son parting with his glory for a season, and humbling himself even to the death of the cross, and doing enough by his death for the salvation of the whole race; but here is the Spirit of truth refusing to work and to put forth his influence upon the souls of multitudes for whom the Saviour died! Behold, my friends, the horrible representation! Transport yourselves, in imagination, to the ancient city, which was crowded with the murderers of our Lord, and see the Saviour weeping over the guilty crowd of infatuated men and women who were madly rushing onwards to an undone eternity. Hear the Saviour uttering, from his inmost soul, the plaintive cry—"O Jerusalem, Jerusalem, thou that killest the prophets, and stonest them which are sent unto thee, how often would I have gathered thy children together, even as a hen gathereth her chickens under her wings, and ye would not!" Mark the emphatic words, "ye would not." It is not, "My Father would not"—it is not, "I would not." I say more—it is not, "The Holy Spirit would not impart to you the needful influence." The sentiment of *Jesus* is, "I would, and God the Father and God the Spirit would, but you have yourselves alone to blame for the rejection of salvation: ye would not—ye will not—come to me that ye might have life." But fancy to yourselves one of our modern theologians, who have mixed up with the water of life the poison of a false and unscriptural fatalism—who have set the writings of Plato, or the ravings of Aristotle side by side with the Word of God, and have learned to say, that "whatsoever comes to pass" must necessarily happen, otherwise men would be far stronger than God, and overthrow the irreversible decree!—fancy to yourselves some of these men side by side with the weeping Saviour, when his heart was bursting and breaking over the wickedness and infatuation of the men and women whom he tend to save;—would *they* not have counselled him to dry up his tears? Would *they* not have enlightened his mind upon the philosophy of the whole plan? Would *they* not have asked him to tell them, whether his tears and lamentations could alter or turn back the Divine decree? Would *they* not have corrected his mistake when he exclaimed, in tenderest and most earnest accents, "Ye would not"? And would *they* not have directed him to the Great Spirit, who sits behind the entire machinery of nature, and whose influence alone was awanting in order to fill the entire city with his followers—whose influence alone was needed in order to transform every blaspheming Jew into a genuine convert, and fill the atmosphere around with the most rapturous hallelujahs and sounds of praise? would *they* not have exclaimed, "Say not to those Jews, 'YE *would not.*' Point them to the Holy Ghost, and say, 'HE *would not,*' because if He would, the decree which binds you down to the necessity of playing your part in this dreadful tragedy would be frustrated and overthrown!"

Men and Brethren, I do this night appeal to you in the name of God, and I ask you to say, whether will you give credit to the weeping Jesus, or will you still abide by the blasphemous dogma of an infidel philosophy which has been artfully engrafted upon the pure and unadulterated Word of God? It is the fatalism of the ancient heathen philosophers, which has been imported into the Christian Church during a dark and backsliding age. The dogma of fatalism was introduced by Satan into the schools of theology, and by mixing up the doctrine of necessity or fatalism with the Word of the living God, the great deceiver of souls has forged a strong and a heavy chain, whereby he leads thousands to destruction. And what has the Church done? She has imported her creed, to a great extent, from the dark bosom of the papacy. Who was Calvin? and who were the Reformers? They were mighty men, it is true, but still they were only men. And what had these men not to do? They had to battle against ten thousand deadly errors. And is it any wonder that they were not a match for every one of them? Consider the dark atmosphere amid which they lived and moved, and the wonder is, not that these mighty men of God brought out of the papacy so much of deadly error; the wonder is that they were the means of exhibiting, in their day and generation, so great a proportion of precious truth. And what, I ask, have the churches of the reformation done since the days of these mighty men? Have they followed up the movement which these reformers began?—have they subjected every doctrine to the scrutiny of the Word of God?—have they put their human creeds into the fining pot, and separated the dross from the pure gold? No. We have verily proved ourselves a race of weak and degenerate men. The children of the reformation have not followed the footsteps of their nobler fathers. We have taken their creeds, and we have set them up as if they were the infallible word of God. And if ever any spark of life has been manifested since the days of the fathers of the reformation, it has been the life which is only the manifestation of spiritual death—the life and the activity of men who arouse themselves to exertion only when it is necessary to expel from their churches those who would presume to question the infallibility of the Confession of Faith!—who would dare to "try all things by the Word of God, and hold fast only that which is good"! There are many of the doctrines in these Confessions which are precious; but who could expect that there should be nothing that is wrong? And I, therefore, earnestly and affectionately call upon you to say, whether you will abide by the words of God himself, and take his assurance and oath, that he withholds nothing from you that is necessary for your salvation; or whether you will take the word of men, when they tell you, that except ye happen to be included in the decree, which the imaginations of infidel philosophers hath conjured into being, the Holy Spirit withholds from you that influence which is indispensable to salvation. Choose ye this day whom ye will believe. If the Lord Jehovah be true, when he swears by himself that he desires your life, believe him; but if fallible men be true when they hold out a dogma which contradicts the oath of Jehovah, believe them.

LECTURE SIXTH.

THIS THEORY OF ELECTION INVOLVES THE DENIAL OF THE NECESSITY OF THE INFLUENCE OF THE HOLY SPIRIT IN ORDER TO CONVERSION—QUOTATIONS FROM MR. HENTON AND DR. WARDLAW.

JOHN vi. 44.—"No man can come to me, except the Father, which hath sent me, draw him."

JOHN ix. 41.—"If ye were blind, ye should have no sin: but now ye say, We see; therefore your sin remaineth."

JOHN iii. 18.—"He that believeth not is condemned already, because he hath not believed in the name of the only-begotten Son of God."

THE verse which has first been read informs us that, without the Holy Spirit, no man can believe; the verse next quoted informs us, that if men could not believe, they would have no sin when they do not exercise faith in Jesus; and the last passage announces the sinfulness of not believing, and ascribes the condemnation of all those who remain condemned to the fact, that they have not believed in the name of the only-begotten Son of God.

Now what is the plain and obvious inference from these indisputable facts? If men cannot believe without the Spirit; and if they would not sin against

God by not believing, if they really could not believe, shall we conclude, that all those from whom the Spirit is withheld are without sin when they do not believe? Such a conclusion as this would evidently be mistaken, because our Saviour plainly tells us, that so flagrant is the sin of unbelief, that it is announced as if it alone constituted the sole and the exclusive ground of condemnation. What, then, are we to make of these plain statements? Are we to attempt to explain them away altogether, or are we to arrive at the conclusion, that the Bible contradicts itself? Nay, verily. Let us rather admit, that no man is commanded to believe without the Spirit, and the entire mystery is solved. No man is required to believe without the Spirit, therefore no man is commanded to do what the Bible expressly declares no man can do. If men could not believe, there would be no sin in their unbelief; but now we say they can believe, therefore their sin remaineth when they do not believe, and for their unbelief they are justly condemned.

III. THE THIRD OBJECTION WHICH WE STATE AGAINST THIS DOCTRINE OF ELECTION IS, THAT IT DOES AWAY WITH THE NECESSITY OF THE INFLUENCE OF THE HOLY SPIRIT TO ENABLE MEN TO BELIEVE.

The grave and heavy charge which I now adduce against this theory of election, I do not mean to substantiate by mere circumstantial evidence or inferential proof. Not that there would exist the slightest difficulty in doing this, so as to make out an unanswerable argument against it, but because, in the first instance at least, it is better at once to remove every shade of doubt or suspicion from your minds, as to the result of the important argument, which, under this head of discourse, we mean to pursue. We shall read to you the published declarations of our brethren themselves. We therefore solicit your attention to the following extracts.

The first is from the second edition of a very able treatise, entitled, "The Work of the Holy Spirit in Conversion, by John Howard Hinton of London." In the ninth page of the advertisement prefixed to that very talented work, the author most candidly and honourably apprises his readers of the great point which he means to establish.

"I have argued [says Mr. Hinton] that our being able to do anything is the same as our having sufficient means of doing it; that we have sufficient means of doing our whole duty without the Holy Spirit; and that, therefore, we are able to do our whole duty without him." P. 9.

Such is this author's own statement of the main doctrine which his work was written and published to support. I shall append to this quotation a single specimen of the argument embodied in the book. The author is trying to prove his position from the Bible, and here is one of his proofs.

"5. In this place, also, we may introduce the passage in which the apostle asserts the intrinsic and independent sufficiency of the divine word: 'From a child thou hast known the Holy Scriptures, *which are able to make thee wise unto salvation*, through faith which is in Christ Jesus.' 2 Tim. iii. 15. We scarcely need stay to prove that the apostle here assigns to the Scriptures a sufficiency to make men wise unto salvation, *apart from the influence of the Holy Spirit.* No reference to the Spirit is contained in the passage or its connexion, nor is there any ground for introducing it. We observe more particularly, that the sufficiency of the Scriptures to impart saving wisdom is not to be viewed in the abstract, but in connexion with the persons to whom they are given: they are *able to make* US *wise unto salvation.* Now this, it is manifest, implies something respecting our condition as well as the excellency of the Scripture itself. It is not able to make an idiot or an infant or a dead man wise unto salvation—it can have this effect upon none but such as are capable of understanding, appreciating, and obeying it—whence it evidently follows that we, whom it is able to make wise unto salvation, are able to understand it, to appreciate and to obey." P. 134.

These are the words of the writer who is looked up to by many as one champion of modern orthodoxy. The brethren whose sentiments are thus expressed and thus defended, are surely themselves denying the necessity of the Spirit's work in order to make men wise unto salvation. We are plainly and expressly informed, that any man, if he be not an idiot or an infant or a dead man, is perfectly able to become wise unto salvation, apart from the influence of the Holy Spirit. And yet these are the theologians who take the lead in charging upon us the denial of the work of the Spirit! We are informed, in the extract which we have just quoted to you, that the apostle says nothing at all about the Holy Spirit in the passage of Scripture on which the doctrine is founded; but we press the simple question, "Does *the apostle say* in that passage what our brethren say, when they tell us that the Scriptures are able to make us wise unto salvation *apart from the influence of the Spirit of God*"? We confidently submit, that the apostle propounds no such doctrine. He does not make mention of the Spirit—that is quite true. But if the apostle does not mention the Holy Spirit, he does not mean thereby to deny and to dishonour him by affirming, or even implying, that men may do very well without him in the matter of their salvation.

Let this erroneous principle of interpretation be carried out, and the very reverse of the assertion may be easily proved. Our brethren say, that men may be saved without the Holy Spirit. Upon their principle of interpretation it would be easy to prove that men may be saved without the Word. Our Saviour said, for example, when he spoke to Nicodemus, "Except a man be born of water, and of the Spirit, he cannot see the kingdom of God." Now if any man has a right to take up the statement of Paul, wherein he asserts, that "the Holy Scriptures are able to make us wise unto salvation," and to argue therefrom that there is no need of the Spirit in order to enable men to be saved, may not another man take up the words of our Lord to Nicodemus, and argue therefrom, that there is no need of the Scriptures in order to lead men to salvation? There is no mention made of the Holy Spirit by Paul. That is true enough. But it is equally true that there is no mention made of the Scriptures by our Lord. And if it may be argued in the one case, that because the Scriptures only are expressly mentioned—therefore men may be saved without the Spirit—may it not be argued in the other case, that there is no need for the Bible at all, for men may be converted by water and the Spirit, which alone are expressly mentioned by our Lord?

The next quotation which I make is from the work of Dr. Wardlaw, from which, in former Lectures, I have freely quoted. The book from which I have already quoted, was written avowedly on the work of the Spirit; the book from which I am now to quote, was written avowedly for the purpose of proving the universal extent of the work of the Son; but in some parts of this book Dr. Wardlaw states his sentiments, and those of others who have adopted his theory of election, and these are precisely the sentiments of the author from whom I have last quoted.

There exists in men universally [says Dr. W.] a ground of responsibility—all that is requisite, as before explained, to render them justly accountable. The accountableness for the treatment they give to the offers of the gospel arises from the nature of those offers themselves, as well as of *human capabilities, irrespectively of all secret purposes in the mind of God, and of all communications of grace to the mind of man.* All to whom the gospel message comes, and who have 'ears to hear,' have the means of salvation in their power; and *it depends on their own will whether salvation is, or is not to be theirs.*"—*Discourses*, p. 180.

The last sentence of this quotation announces a most delightful truth. One would imagine, at first sight, that there is implied in it, *in the first place*, the admission that there is no secret purpose unconditionally decreeing any man to inevitable destruction; and, *in the second place*, that the gracious influence of the Spirit, without which no man can come to Jesus, and whereby the Father draws us, is not withheld from any. But to our unspeakable astonishment, we are here arrested by the information that such is by no means true. We refer you to the context, where we are reminded of the secret purpose and the special influence! We are told that the reason why it depends upon the will of men whether or not salvation may be theirs, arises from man's perfect capability to believe, in direct opposition to God's eternal purpose and the Holy Spirit's indispensable grace! To this doctrine we cannot subscribe. For what is this but to set up man's power—to exhibit what is styled man's "capabilities"—as something stronger than the decree of God! What is this but to assert that man wants only the will to prove himself more than a match for the overthrow of the counsels and decrees of the Almighty! What is this but to inform us that the sinner has no need whatever of any influence of the Spirit, but is perfectly competent to save himself even to the overthrow of the throne of the eternal God!

I have now done what, in this discourse, I purposed to do. I have laid before you the proof, that I prefer no false or groundless charge against brethren, when I discard their theory of election, because it leads to a denial of the necessity of the Spirit's influence in order to enable sinners to believe.

And now, my fellow-sinners, permit me again, in parting from you, to remind you, affectionately and solemnly, of the oath of your God. "As I live, saith the Lord God, I have no pleasure in the death of the wicked, but that the wicked turn from his way and live: turn ye, turn ye, from your evil ways, for why will ye die?" In parting from you again, I point you to that oath, and I ask you, Is God sincere and honest even when he swears? I point you to more than to his oath—behold the sacrifice of his Son! Sinner, behold the Lamb of God bearing away the sins of the world! Sinner, thy sins were all laid upon that innocent and spotless sacrifice! They are all away—away from between thee and thy God—away from between thee and the blessed influence of the Spirit, who, even now, is wooing every prodigal here back again to God! "Behold, I stand at the door and knock." Thus the Holy Spirit strives! But he will not strive for ever. Death, judgment, eternity—these are at the door, and if the Spirit part from you at death, he parts with you for ever.

LECTURE SEVENTH.

THE NECESSITY OF THE INFLUENCE OF THE HOLY SPIRIT TO ENABLE MEN TO BELIEVE—SEMI-ORTHODOX PREACHING—QUOTATION FROM DR. WARDLAW—NATURAL AND MORAL INABILITY.

JOHN iii. 5.—"Jesus answered, Verily, verily, I say unto thee, Except a man be born of water and of the Spirit, he cannot enter into the kingdom of God."

JOHN vi. 44.—"No man can come to me, except the Father, which hath sent me, draw him: and I will raise him up at the last day."

HERE, then, are two Scripture witnesses, whose testimony we hesitate not to set in opposition to the two fallible witnesses whose report has been listened to in our previous discourse. The one witness declares that no man can come to Christ, or believe in him, without the drawing of the Father; the other witness declares that a sinner cannot see the kingdom of God, or be converted or born again, apart from the influence of the Spirit. These two statements of the Word of God are thus express and definite in their testimony in support of the absolute necessity of the Spirit to enable any man to believe.

Now we crave your attention to the one single point which needs here to be examined. It is not denied by any man who supports the doctrine to which we now object, that the Spirit of God is needed to make the sinner *willing* to believe. And so, when we come to state such passages of Scripture in opposition to their doctrine, they explain away their import by affirming, that the only want experienced by men is a want of will. And so they would paraphrase the two Scripture proofs now under examination in the following way:—"No man *will* come to me, except the Father, who hath sent me, draw him," although any man and every man is quite able to believe in me without the drawing of the Father. And again, "Except a man be born of the Spirit, he *will* not see the kingdom of God," although any man has power enough to be born again, and to see the kingdom of God, and to enjoy its privileges without the Spirit!!!

Here, then, is the single point which you will require to keep before your minds, in order that you may arrive at a just and intelligent decision. Does the inability of men to believe, or to be born again into the family of God, without the Spirit, amount to a mere want of will and nothing more? The question is not, whether the sinner is naturally unwilling to believe—that is not the question, for that is most fully admitted. But granting that he is unwilling, the question remains, Has he perfect power to believe and be saved without the influence of the Spirit, so that he is able to become wise unto salvation, without any interposition on the part of the third person of the Godhead? Now, in answer to this question, we request you to observe, and to remember well, the distinct assertions of the Word of God to which we have referred you; and we ask you, without any prejudice in your minds, to decide as to their plain and common-sense import. When you read the words, "No man can come to me except the Father draw him," do you suppose, as honest and unprejudiced men and women, that you are at liberty to interpret these words so as to infer that any man is perfectly able to come to Jesus without the drawing of the Father? Would not such an interpretation amount to a contradiction of our Saviour's statement? And when you read the words, "Except a man be born of the Spirit, he cannot see the kingdom of God," would any of you think of saying, that you were bringing out the meaning of the solemn and emphatic declaration, by asserting that any man is perfectly able to see the kingdom of God without the Spirit? Yet such is the interpretation which is put upon such statements!! It is affirmed that such passages of Scripture do not assert a want of power on the part of the sinner to do well enough without the Spirit, but that they refer, simply and exclusively, to a want of will to exercise his powers in the right and proper direction. And we are referred to the obvious fact, that the Holy Spirit, in conversion, does not impart to the sinner any new faculties or powers of mind, and brethren erroneously conclude, that because the sinner does not get a set of new faculties or powers when he is converted, that therefore he is able to convert himself without the Spirit!!

The error to which we now advert arises from an oversight of the fact, that the reason why every man is able to believe is, that every man is, in point of fact, drawn by God with the view of bringing him to the acceptance of a full and free salvation. But suppose that any sinner were not drawn by God, we submit that it would be impossible for him *(even though he were willing)* to believe in Jesus. We submit that, while every man is able to come with the drawing, and in consequence of the drawing, of the Father, no man is able to come, or could possibly be able to come without this drawing influence; and we hold that, when any man resolves this want of ability to be saved without the Spirit into a mere want of will, he is perverting and setting aside the infallible statements of the infallible Word.

We may here illustrate our doctrine by a parallel case. Take the supposition of a mighty prince, in a remote province of whose dominions the standard of rebellion has been erected, but who has resolved, in virtue of a satisfaction given to his government, to proclaim, in person, a free pardon to every one of his rebel subjects. You must suppose that the minds of the rebels are filled with hard and suspicious thoughts respecting their lawful sovereign. They know his power, but they are impressed with the idea that he is desirous only to exercise his power in oppressing and punishing them for their rebellion. He might send forth an ambassador to proclaim a pardon to the rebels and to invite them back again to their allegiance. But he takes a different plan. He leaves his splendid palace; he goes forth himself with his own proclamation, and he himself announces it in person to the rebels; he goes in person from city to city, and from town to town, and from village to village, and from house to house; he announces, with his own lips, to every one of his rebel subjects the wonderful intelligence, that his own son—the heir of his kingdom and his throne—has voluntarily subjected himself to punishment in their room and stead; he announces to them the farther intelligence, that so desirous was he himself for their happiness, that he accepted of the substitution, of his son and heir in their stead, for the very purpose of enabling him consistently to offer them a free pardon, and save them from the punishment which their revolt had justly merited; he entreats and beseeches and implores the rebels, on his bended knees, to lay down their arms and submit to his government, and not to compel him, most reluctantly, to execute summary vengeance upon them, by persisting any longer in their rebellion! The result of all this personal entreaty is, that some of the rebels become subdued in their enmity by the wondrous condescension of the sovereign, and submit themselves to his sway, while the rest of them will not believe him, nor give him credit for his generosity and kindness, and therefore remain rebels, and are consequently treated as enemies, simply because they refuse to be reconciled.

In this case you will perceive, that the only reason why any one of these rebel subjects are not saved from the consequences of their revolt, is, that they *will not* believe and trust the kindness of their sovereign, and refuse, consequently, to be at peace with him. It would be absurd to say that on such a supposition they *could not* believe. It was simply because they would not, and not because they could not. The self-same influence which was brought to bear upon those rebels who were induced to accept the pardon of their prince, was brought to bear upon those who obstinately persisted in their revolt, shutting their ears against the entreaties, and their eyes against the manifested kindness of their most gracious sovereign. The only difference between the two classes of individuals consisted in this—the one yielded to the drawing influence of their sovereign's compassionate efforts, the other resisted the same drawing influence which was exerted equally upon them, with the view of winning them back to their allegiance.

But if you *alter the supposition*, and imagine to yourselves the sovereign of whom we have spoken, selecting from among these rebel subjects a few special favourites, and passing by all the rest, and condescending to visit in person only those houses or cities that happen to be inhabited by the favoured few—you entirely change the whole aspect of the case. You thereby render it absolutely impossible for the rebels who are passed by to believe in the gracious intentions of their sovereign—to accept his pardon, and to become reconciled to his person and his government. In the case already supposed, it was possible for them to be reconciled, and it was sinful for them to remain in a position of hostility, because the drawing influence of their sovereign's kindness was exerted equally upon them all. They had all of them evidence sufficient to convince them, and motive sufficient to induce them, to lay down their arms and be at peace. But in the case now supposed, they want the evidence necessary to convince them, and the motive necessary to induce them, and it is not because they have not the use of all their powers or faculties, but because they cannot possibly exercise their powers in the way of believing, without any evidence, or changing their minds without any motive, that it is utterly impossible for them to accept the pardon which the sovereign most graciously proclaims. In this case, what does the sovereign do? He passes them by—he does not condescend to speak to them—he does not deign to notice them. He knocks at the door of their neighbour's house—he repairs to the gate of the adjoining city—and he pleads with his favourites, and his favourites alone. The rebels who are passed by do not, of course, believe that there is any pardon for them. They do not believe that their sovereign desires them to be at peace with him. They believe, on the other hand, that all that the man wants is, to get his pampered favourites induced to flee with him out of the scene of revolt, and that his determination is only the more unalterably fixed to take summary vengeance on all the rest, and in due time visit them, if he can, with fire and sword. They do not believe in his love to them, and they are not reconciled.

Now, the question which I propose to you is this—Whether is it because the men will not believe, or because they cannot believe, in the love of their sovereign to them that they remain rebels? Mark well the true position of affairs. The king passes by their door. He does not pass them by because he has no time to visit them. He does not pass them by because he falls into the mistake of ignorance, and does not know that their houses are inhabited. He came to the rebel province with an unalterable determination not to speak to them at all. Nay more, he knew that he needed only to pass them by in order to confirm and harden them in their rebellion; and because he determined to destroy them, he passed them by. This is what the men are told. This is what they are taught to believe. I ask any man of common sense to tell me, if, in this case, it be possible for the men to believe in the pardoning mercy of their prince, and to be reconciled? The visit of the king to his special favourites, is not, in this case, fitted to draw the rest; it is fitted to repel them. This special influence put forth upon some, it is evident, is not a drawing, but a repelling influence to all the rest. They cannot—it is not that they will not, but it is an absolute impossibility for them to believe in their sovereign's love, because the sovereign does not seek to draw them.

The preachers of our day who hold the theory now under examination, preach a gospel to all men; but they tell all men, at the same time, that God has unalterably determined that all from whom the special influence is withheld are doomed by God to unconditional damnation. Here, then, is the evidence—the only evidence which is presented before perishing thousands, Sabbath after Sabbath, and year after year. The question is very simple. Is it possible for any man to believe in the face of this evidence in the love of God to his soul, before he is quite sure that the special influence has visited him? It is perfectly plain, on their own principles, that until a man not only has the supposed special influence, but knows infallibly that he has it, the man would be believing in opposition to the plainest evidence, if he ventured to believe in the pardoning mercy of God as bringing to him a free salvation. But it is not possible for any man to believe in opposition to apprehended proof. It is not possible for a man, for example, to believe that it is midnight in the midst of the clearly perceived light of the meridian sun. If any man, therefore, believe that all are doomed to damnation who have not the thing which men call a special influence, he cannot, *in the absence* of that supposed influence from his soul, believe that salvation has come *to him.* It is, therefore, not only unscriptural, but absurd, in the supporters of a special influence, to maintain that any sinner is able to believe and to do all his duty without the Holy Spirit.

I am about to exhibit a specimen of such *semi-orthodox* preaching, from the "*Discourses on the Nature and Extent of the Atonement,*" by Dr. Wardlaw of Glasgow.

I may only premise, that it lacks but one element—the recognition of the necessity of the Holy Spirit's indispensable influence. This will appear very clearly at the close of this quotation.

"If there were a want of natural capacity for believing, there would be equally a want of natural capacity for disbelieving. If there were not this kind of ability to believe, there would be no guilt in unbelief.—O my fellow-sinners, deceive not yourselves, as multitudes have done before you, with this plea of *inability*. The plea is often advanced with a levity of spirit, that sufficiently indicates its origin. 'We cannot, it seems, help ourselves,'—many have thought and said,—'we have no ability to do anything; we cannot change our own hearts; we cannot atone for our sins; we cannot come to God; we cannot believe;—it is divine power, divine grace, that must do the work;—it is not ours;—and if God is not pleased to put forth the necessary power,—what can we do?—There is no help for us:—we must be damned!'—And with the last fearful link of the chain there is secretly associated a self-flattering hope,—a hope founded in the unreasonableness and unrighteousness of such a doom,—that it shall *not* be so. This, I apprehend, is uniformly involved in the real or affected carelessness with which the conclusion,—a conclusion in itself so unspeakably fearful,—is usually uttered. The mind rests its hope secretly on the *unfairness* that *inability should incur condemnation*. The inward surmise is:—'if we really are unable, then every effort of ours must be unavailing; perdition is entailed upon us, and by nothing that we can do is it avoidable:—and yet—and yet —*is this justice?*—and—if it be not justice, *can it be true?*'

"Now, my fellow-sinners, this is all delusion. I come to the point at once; and, with all diffidence, yet with all confidence, I say to you,—if there were no ability, it would *not* be justice. But in the sense in which you urge the plea, and in which, perhaps, it has been put into your lips, there is no truth in it. In the sense in which you plead inability,—the only sense in which the plea could be of any avail,—you are *not* unable. So far from being unable in any sense that even palliates your unbelief and impenitence,—your *inability*, rightly interpreted, resolves itself into the strongest mode of expressing your culpability and guilt. For what does the word mean?—simply, the *strength of your antipathy to God and to goodness.* Your inability to believe is only another phrase for your aversion to the truth of God. Your inability to 'repent, and turn to God, and do works meet for repentance,' what else is it, less or more, than your fondness for the service of sin and of the world, and your unwillingness to relinquish it?—what is it, but that you cannot give up the world;—you cannot renounce your favourite sins;—you cannot abandon 'the lust of the flesh, the lust of the eyes, and the pride of life;' or you cannot bear the mortification of pride, the renunciation of your own righteousness, the crucifixion of self?—What is there in your *cannot*, but the want of *will?*—If you tell me you are *willing* but *not able*, you tell me what never has been, and never can be; what involves, indeed, a flat and palpable contradiction; inasmuch as, the inability affirmed in Scripture being unwillingness, and nothing else whatever, it amounts to neither more nor less than saying that you are willing and unwilling at the same time. To say you *would* believe if you *could*,—is not only not true; it is the precise opposite of truth. The plain truth is, that you *could* believe if you *would;* there being no one thing whatever that prevents you from believing, but the *want of will;* nothing between you and pardon but the want of will to have it in God's way,—that is, freely, and in connexion with holiness, with newness of life.—'I would but can't believe,'—'I would but can't repent,'—are, both of them, as unsound philosophy as they are unsound divinity. If in any instance either were true, there would, in that instance, be no guilt in unbelief and impenitence. It is the will that is wanting, and the will only. The will to believe is, virtually, faith; the will to repent is, virtually, penitence. There never has been the will to either, where there have not actually been both.

"In making the atonement, and in offering you pardon on account of it, if you are willing to accept the pardon on that ground, God has put the blessing in your power. Who is to blame, if you have it not? Not He assuredly; but yourselves, and yourselves alone.—*What would you have?* You have all the natural faculties and powers, that are necessary to constitute a ground of accountableness. You have the natural powers required for considering, understanding, believing, choosing, loving and hating, speaking and acting;—and moreover for asking. The question, then, is, How comes it that these powers are not occupied about proper objects?—how comes it that they are not rightly directed?—Take them in order. You have the power of *considering:*—why is it that you do not consider the 'things that belong to your everlasting peace,'—the things which, of all others, you cannot but be sensible, ought, both in duty and in interest, to be considered by you?—You have the power of *understanding!*—how is it, that you do not understand the divine testimony;—that is, that you do not perceive and appreciate its excellence, and its adaptation both to God's character and to man's need? 'Why, even of yourselves, judge ye not that which is right?'—You have the power of *believing,*—of crediting what is attested by sufficient evidence. You are practising this every day and every hour, on other subjects. How is it, that you do not believe the Word of God,—the glorious gospel,—'the word of reconciliation,' of peace with God through the atoning blood of the cross? Is it because you have examined its evidence, and satisfactorily proved it untrue? or is it because, in its humbling and holy character, it is not to your liking? Let conscience give a faithful answer. You have the power of *choosing:*—you are exercising it continually. How is it, that you do not, among the objects presented for your selection, 'choose the good part that shall never be taken from you?' You have the natural power of *loving,* and of *hating:*—how is it, that you do not love God, love Christ, love holiness?—and how is it, that you do not hate sin, and 'abhor that which is evil'?—how is it that your love and your hatred are not in harmony with those of God, that you do not hate what he hates, and love what he loves? You have the natural power of *speaking* and *acting*;—why is it, that you do not always speak and act aright? I have added to all these—You have the power of *asking*;—yes; and with the power, you have the liberty, in the quarter where most it behoves you to apply; and more even than liberty—earnest invitation, and all the encouragement of faithful promise:—how is it, then, that you do not ask of God?—how is it that you come not to him for the influences of his Spirit, and for the blessings of his salvation? how is it, that, when these blessings are set before you, on the ground of the atonement, in all their fulness and in all their freeness, you do not eagerly and gratefully accept them? —that when the way is opened to the mercy-seat, through the rending of the vail even the Redeemer's flesh, you do not press towards it?—that when 'in Christ's reconciling the world unto himself,' he beseeches you to be reconciled to him, you do not catch with all avidity at the gracious entreaty, and come into friendship with your justly offended God?—O delude not your own souls by talking of *inability*. Is there any other answer that can truly, in the tribunal of conscience, be given to such questions, but one—that you have '*no heart*' to these things —to the truths, to the ways, to the service, or to the enjoyment of God? And if this aversion of heart, this perverseness of disposition, this want of will to that which is good, be not sinful, then is there no such thing as sin in the universe—no moral evil or criminal desert—nothing on account of which any creature can be condemned or punished.

"I again ask, *what would you have?* Every consideration that is calculated to influence and determine the choice of your mind, is set before you;—everything fearful on the one side, everything truly desirable on the other. The terrors of coming wrath are depicted, to induce you to flee from them, and effect a timely escape; and the way of escape is set open before you. All that is, or ought to be, attractive, in the beauties of holiness,—in the prospect of 'fulness of joy and pleasures for evermore,'—in a God who 'delighteth in mercy,' and whose very nature is 'love,'—in a Saviour as willing as he is able, and as able as he is willing, to 'save you to the uttermost,'—in an atonement whose infinite virtue is for all,—in the forgiveness of sin, fellowship with God, and the reciprocations of mutual love between the renewed soul and the divine source of all blessing;—in all that is comprehended in life eternal!—*What would you have?* The most sincere and earnest invitations are addressed to you, assuring you of the divine readiness to receive and to bless you: and every one of these invitations proceeds upon the assumption, that there is nothing between you and the enjoyment of the blessings to which you are invited, but *your own will.* Jehovah—the God with whom it is impossible to lie, swears to you by the certainty and necessity of his own being—'As I live, I have no pleasure in the death of the wicked, but rather that the wicked turn from his wicked way, and live: turn ye, turn ye, for why will ye die?' and Jesus, the divine Saviour, pleads with, and entreats, and encourages you—'Come unto me, all ye that labour and are heavy-laden, and I will give you rest.'—*What would you have?* What more is necessary to constitute a valid ground of responsibility?—think,—and say,—what more is there required?—what is wanting?—There is nothing remaining, that I can conceive of, but your being *made willing.* Will you say that *this* is necessary to your accountableness? If you wish to retain your claim to rationality, you will never advance such a plea. Think a moment—a moment will be enough—of its self-contradictory absurdity: that it should be necessary for you to be *made willing,* in order to your becoming accountable for being *unwilling!*—that a right disposition requires to be imparted, in order to your being responsible for cherishing and indulging a wrong one! And yet, gross as is the absurdity of the sentiment, it is greatly to be feared that some impious surmise of this kind floats in many minds—that unless God give them a right disposition, *they cannot help it.* But the entire Bible proceeds on the assumption that the wrong disposition is your sin,—existing and operating wilfully, resisting the inducements to its suppression and crucifixion, and neither desiring nor seeking divine aid to effect it.—*What would you have?* You are neither compelled to evil, nor forcibly restrained from good. You voluntarily choose the one; you voluntarily refuse the other. It is a matter of consciously spontaneous preference. *What, then,* I still urge upon you, *would you have?* You cannot be saved against your will. You cannot have your hearts changed against your will. You cannot be made willing against your will! You have all the powers before enumerated: you have all conceivable motives presented to you to exercise those powers aright—in the choice, the love, the pursuit, and the enjoyment of right and worthy objects: you are under no compulsory and no withholding power. Why, then, I repeat, do you remain at a distance from God, when he invites you to his presence and his favour? Why are you not interested in the virtue of the atonement, when you are assured that its virtue is free to you and to all? Why are you not partakers of the blessings of God's salvation, when these, in all the free munificence of the Godhead, are set before you, and pressed upon your acceptance? Why are you not in the way to heaven, when the gate is thrown wide, and entrance not permitted merely but urged? *Who,* let me ask, or *what,* prevents you? WHO? *Not God:* he invites, entreats, prays you, and, with the sceptre of his grace extended, waits for you, that you may touch it, and live. *Not Christ.* He has shed his blood for sinners, and for you among the rest,—he sets himself before you, crucified and slain—he shows you his hands and his side, and says, 'Him that cometh unto me I will in no wise cast out.' WHAT, then, prevents you? Nothing whatever, in the form of obstacle, lies in your way, save those which are thrown there by the devil, the world, and the flesh, operating upon your earthly and corrupt affections, and indisposing you to leave the broad way and enter the narrow; that is, there is nothing but the strong antagonist power of your inclination to sense and sin. The sole obstacle is to be found in the words—'*Ye will not.*' Do not delude yourselves by fancying there is anything else. Cheat not your souls with words. Believe not those who would lay your consciences to sleep on the pillow of an imaginary inability. Unwillingness is the word. It is the inability of disinclination—of alienation of heart; *moral* inability. You *can*, but *will not*, is the truth; or, if you like it better, though it is the same thing, you cannot, *because* you will not." —Pp. 146–155.

I have now done with the reading of the quotation, and I have one question to propose—Do you not perceive the important, the *studied* omission? The excellent author, from whose discourses we have read, is true to *his system*. But what has become of *the special influence*, for which he contends so zealously, and which he believes to be the saving influence of the Holy Spirit? What has he made of *this?* Is there any reference to its necessity, or to the necessity of the Spirit of God in any form, or in any degree whatever, in order to the conversion of the sinner to God? It is painful, indeed, to differ on a point so very important from such a writer as this. But is it possible to agree, even with this revered servant of Jesus Christ, without committing ourselves to *a denial* of the necessity of Divine influence in order to the production of saving faith? He asks—"*Who* or *what* prevents you?" And mark his reply—"*Not God:* he invites, entreats, prays you; and, with the sceptre of his grace extended, waits for you, that you may touch it, and live. *Not Christ.* He has shed his blood for sinners, and for you among the rest—he sets himself before you, crucified and slain—he shows you his hands and his side, and says, 'Him that cometh unto me, I will in no wise cast out.' *What*, then, prevents you?" Our answer to this question is, "*The Holy Spirit's blessed influence is awanting still.*" Is it possible that this writer could pen and preach the beautiful and striking appeal to sinners which we have quoted, and not *think* of this most important omission? Would that Dr. Wardlaw had added one single sentence more, just before asking the sinner, "*What*, then, prevents you?" Would that he had written down such a sentence as this—"*Not the Holy Spirit:* for thus it is written, 'To-day, *as the Holy Ghost saith*, to-day, Oh that ye would hear his voice, and harden not your hearts.' And again, '*The Spirit*, as well as the Bride, says Come.' And, yet once more, every moment you remain unconverted, 'Ye do always *resist the Holy Ghost.*'" Would Dr. Wardlaw have compromised *his system*, had he appended such a sentence as this? Doubtless he would, and *he knew it.* But does not this only prove, even to a demonstration, that this system lacks "*one thing needful*" to be consistent with the Word of God—the recognition of the absolute necessity of *the influence of the Spirit*, in order to enable any sinner to believe in Christ, and to be saved? We pause for a reply.

We shall doubtless be referred to the distinction between natural and moral inability—a distinction which our brethren are in the habit of drawing with the view of evading the difficulty in which they are placed by their theory, and escaping the consequences to which it inevitably leads. Justice, therefore, to our subject, requires us to examine this point, before dismissing this part of our argument.

What do brethren understand by *moral* and what by *natural* ability? The former implies the possession of the power or ability *to will*. The latter implies the possession of the power *to act*. It is admitted on all hands that the action is dependent upon the will. So dependent is the action upon the will, and so closely connected are they with each other, that, in the passage now quoted, Dr. Wardlaw says, that "the will to believe is virtually faith; the will to repent is virtually penitence. There never has been the will to either, where there have not actually been both." This is a very strong assertion of what is called man's *natural ability* to believe unto salvation. But while it is asserted that wherever there is the will to believe, faith is the invariable result, it is evidently, indeed necessarily, implied that faith cannot exist where the will to believe is awanting. Where the will exists, faith is said invariably to follow. But where the will is awanting faith will be admitted, as a matter of course, to be impossible. "You *could* believe if you *would*," Dr. Wardlaw says. But it is no less true that you *cannot* believe, if you *will not*. The second statement is no less true than the first. They stand or fall together. But it is affirmed that men have not the power to will. This is affirmed by our brethren who have unanswerably demonstrated, and who glory in admitting, that men have the power to believe. Let us inquire, therefore, into the reason of their strong assertion of man's power to believe. We take the statement of the excellent author from whom we have so largely quoted. He says truly—"if there were no ability it would not be justice" to condemn any sinner on the ground of unbelief. Here, then, is one strong position which we occupy in asserting man's perfect ability savingly to believe. The responsibility of the sinner is measured by his opportunity or his power. But the question arises—is the sinner not responsible for his determinations or volitions? Is he not responsible for the manner in which he exercises his will? Listen again to Dr. Wardlaw's reply to this question—"If this aversion of heart—this perverseness of disposition—this want of will to that which is good, be not sinful, then is there no such thing as sin in the universe—no moral evil or criminal desert—nothing, on account of which any creature can be condemned or punished." Here again we have the happiness of saying amen to the doctrine of Dr. Wardlaw. It is sinful—justly punishable—not to will in accordance with the will of God. Now comes our inquiry—why is the sinner justly punishable for not *willing* to believe? Will Dr. Wardlaw *here* withdraw his words—"*If there were no ability it would not be justice*"? Surely not. The assertion is just, and it is true that the measure of a man's ability is the measure of his responsibility. But every man is responsible for the direction in which he *wills*. On Dr. Wardlaw's own principle, therefore, the sinner must possess *the power—the ability* to will. It is upon the admission of this truth, and that alone, that our brethren can maintain their consistency. They cannot surely argue that it would be unjust in God to condemn the sinner who has no power to believe, because the man believes not; and at the same time affirm that it is perfectly just in God to condemn the sinner who has no power to will because he wills not! If the want of power be the measure of just responsibility in the one case—it is the same in the other case. And therefore we submit with all deference to the venerated man from whom we have quoted, that the same principle whereby he establishes man's natural ability to believe, proves beyond all reasonable question, that the sinner possesses the power or the ability to will, as well as the power or ability to do, consistently with the just and righteous command of God.

You must have noticed that, in the quotation already made, even Dr. Wardlaw expresses himself upon this point with evident inconsistency. He speaks, in the first place, as if any man in his senses ever dreamt of maintaining the absurdity that *a sinner must be willing before he can be responsible for being unwilling!* Did the doctor ever listen to the assertion of an absurdity such as this beyond the precincts of an asylum? Nay, verily. He accordingly says very truly, "If you wish to retain your claim *to rationality,* you will never advance such a plea. Think a moment—a moment will be enough—of its self-contradictory absurdity: that it should be necessary for you to be *made willing* in order to your becoming accountable for being *unwilling!*" The doctor is verily right in affirming that no *sane* man could possibly advance such a plea. "And yet, gross as is the absurdity of the sentiment, it is greatly to be feared [adds this writer] that some impious surmise of this kind floats in many minds—that unless God give them a right disposition, *they cannot help it.*" Is it possible that Dr. Wardlaw could purposely set himself to practise a deception upon the minds of his readers? It is impossible. It is therefore very evident that the doctor is himself labouring under a gross misconception, when he confounds *the act of willing* with *the power to will.* It is absurd, indeed, to imagine, even for a moment, that the actual existence of the former is essential to responsibility; but it is not absurd to affirm that a man is not, and cannot be, justly held responsible, if the latter be indeed awanting. But any ignorant and unthinking individual who should happen to peruse or listen to the eloquent appeal of this writer, would imagine, and would be warranted to infer from the expressions we have quoted, that the doctor's opponents must be irrational indeed! No man could imagine for a moment that the doctor is capable of descending to an *intentional* misrepresentation; and few men have been accustomed to observe the egregious blunders into which even great and learned men constantly fall, when they are warped and entangled by an absurd and erroneous system of theology. And knowing that Dr. Wardlaw is morally incapable of misrepresentation, and fancying, moreover, that HE is intellectually incapable of falling into a very ridiculous mistake—most of his readers will doubtless imagine that the system which he aims at in the expressions now under consideration, actually proceeds upon the absurd conception, that the sinner must be "*made willing*" before he can be responsible for being unwilling! The followers of Dr. Wardlaw would be surprised, indeed, if Dr. Candlish or Dr. Marshall, or any of the extreme men of Calvin, should try to argue against Dr. Wardlaw's strong assertion of every sinner's ability to believe, so that, "*if there were no ability it would not be justice*" to condemn him for unbelief, in the same style as Dr. Wardlaw has attempted to argue against the sinner's ability to will. What if Dr. Wardlaw should be met by the following statements in the form of a refutation :—"If you, Dr. Ralph Wardlaw, wish to retain your claim to rationality, you will never advance such a plea. Think a moment—a moment will be enough—of its self-contradictory absurdity: that it should be necessary for you to be *made to believe*, in order to your becoming accountable for your *unbelief!* And yet, gross as is the absurdity of the sentiment, it is evident from your book that some impious surmise of this kind floats in your mind—that unless God constrain you to believe, *it would not be justice to condemn you.*" Would Dr. Wardlaw or his followers in his own Union, and also in the United Presbyterian Church, be satisfied with such a representation of their own sentiments? Would they not be very ready to detect the fallacy and cry out against the injustice? Would they not exclaim—"We never said that the sinner needed to be *made to believe*, but that the sinner must possess *the power to believe* before he can be justly punished for his unbelief; and you, Doctors Candlish and Marshall, confound *the act of believing* with *the power* to believe, and you thus misrepresent our doctrine when you try to fasten upon it such an absurdity"?—Would not this be Dr. Wardlaw's reply to such an argument against his own doctrine—"that a man is not responsible for not believing who wants the power to believe"? Such, then, is *our* reply to *his* argument against our doctrine, when we maintain "that a man is not responsible for being unwilling who wants the power to will."

The ground occupied by Dr. Wardlaw, when he affirms that God cannot justly condemn any sinner for unbelief who has not the power to believe, is the exact foundation on which any man may take his stand and maintain the injustice of condemning any sinner for *not willing* to believe who wants the power to will. It is not the want of *faith* which would render it unjust in God to punish, but the want *of power* to exercise faith. How absurd to imagine that a man *must have* faith before he can be justly punished for *the want* of it! But does *Dr. Wardlaw* entertain such an absurd notion as this? He does, if his argument be worth anything, when he exclaims, "How absurd to imagine that a man *must have* the will to believe before he can be justly punished for the want of will!" Both absurdities are equally absurd. But if the last is necessarily implied in the doctrine, that *the power to will* is necessary to responsibility for unwillingness, the first is equally implied in the doctrine, that *the power to believe* is necessary to responsibility for unbelief. But Dr. Wardlaw does not entertain such an absurdity as that a man must *believe* in order to be justly punished for *not believing!* His argument, therefore, is not worth a straw against us when he speaks of "the self-contradictory absurdity—that it should be necessary for you to be *made willing* in order to your becoming accountable for being *unwilling!*" The doctor has evidently been aiming at some system which has no "claim to rationality," when he penned the sentences we have been examining. But we humbly submit, that the implied charge falls back upon his own theory. It is surely most irrational to affirm, that the want of power to discharge one obligation releases the sinner from just responsibility, while it is, at the same time, maintained, that the same want of power to discharge another obligation leaves the man accountable for its neglect. But the theory now under examination admits the injustice of punishing a man for not believing aright if the man wants the power to believe, while it affirms that there is *no injustice* whatever in punishing a man for not willing aright if the man wants the power to will!! Is not *this* inconsistent and irrational?

But no stronger reasoning can be advanced in favour of the vaunted distinction between natural and moral ability and inability. It is a distinction without a difference, and no solid argument can be based upon it. The self-same argument which establishes what is called man's natural ability, or power to believe and to do his duty, demonstrates man's moral ability or power *to will*, to believe, and to do his duty. And the same weapon whereby the one should be overthrown would destroy both, and that, too, at the same stroke.

Any man who peruses the long extract which we have quoted from Dr. Wardlaw might be led to inquire, whether the doctor *seriously* believes the theory which he has set himself to maintain. Does the doctor not assure the sinner, that he has the power not only of considering, understanding, believing, but also of "*choosing*"? To this we say, amen. But what says *the system* which is based upon the imaginary distinction between natural and moral ability—the system which affirms that man has no power of choice? Have I not quoted the doctor's express words, when I have written down the following—"*What would you have?* You are neither compelled to evil, nor forcibly restrained from good. You voluntarily choose the one; you voluntarily refuse the other. It is a matter of *consciously spontaneous* preference. *What then,* I still urge upon you, *would you have?* You cannot be saved against your will. You cannot have your hearts changed against your will! You cannot be made willing against your will! You have all the powers before enumerated." And now we again ask, Has not Dr. Wardlaw himself expressly mentioned, among the number of man's natural powers, *the power of choice?* And what is the power to choose but the power to determine or to will in one direction rather than in any other? And has not the doctor appealed to every man's *consciousness* in support of this great truth? And if, in support of this great truth, every man's consciousness decides, what have we but an infallible decision *against the system* which affirms the want of the power to will or to choose in the absence of a special influence for which this writer has been wont to contend?

When it is demanded of us now, "*What, then, would you have?*" we think we are fully warranted to reply, "*We would have the honest consistency of truthful and truth-loving men.*" We would have anything rather than a system of shuffling and shifting and popularity-hunting *expediency*. We would have a consistent advocacy of the glorious and soul-saving truth by brethren *who have much to answer for* at the judgment-seat of God, seeing that to whomsoever much talent and much influence is given, of them much shall be required. We would have the esteemed and eloquent writer from whom we have quoted, and our very esteemed friends of the United Presbyterian Church, to lead forward and advance the mighty movement which has been begun in our land, instead of frowning upon it and retarding it, and doing all in their power to crush and annihilate it. Or, if we cannot have this, we would have the opposite consistent alternative. Let them stand by Dr. Marshall and his party. Let us have the consistency of error rather than this truckling and halting expediency, and we shall know how to deal with it. But when we have at one time, and in one sentence, the confession of the truth, and, in the very next sentence or discourse, the exhibition of opposing error; when now we have Jesus Christ, and, in a short time, John Calvin, exhibited as an authority; when we have, in one page, the assertion that man has no power to will without the special, indefinable, irresistible influence of an ideal theology, and, in another page, the affirmation of man's perfect power to will as well as to believe, without the Holy Spirit at all; when we have the one or the other —error or truth, truth or error, or truth *and* error, both together, jumbled and hashed up in one heterogeneous mass, precisely as expediency may direct;—when we have such a state of things round about us, we are almost confounded by the question, which is again and again pressed upon our notice,—"*What would you have?*"

But the plea which is founded upon the distinction between natural and moral inability, is evidently unsound and untenable, not only for the reason already stated, but for another reason, with the statement of which we shall now conclude this discourse. It is admitted that men cannot be saved against their will, or have their hearts changed against their will, or consider, or ask, or perform one single duty against their will; and yet they are informed by these sapient teachers, that they have the power to believe and to be saved, while they are at the same time warned not to believe "*the heresy*" which assures them that they possess the power to will! Without their will, they are not able to believe or to do their duty, but they are quite able to believe and to do their whole duty, although they have no power or command over their will! Is not this a palpable absurdity? How can sinners be possessed of natural ability, or the power to act aright, if they have no power to will aright, when the doing is admittedly dependent upon the previous willing? How is it possible for any man to take the second step, when it is not possible for him so much as to attempt the first step, it being admitted that the former is necessarily dependent upon the latter? Does not this absurd philosophy mar the beauty, and take the heart and soul out of the glorious gospel, with which it has been unnaturally linked? What is the gospel which our brethren present, Sabbath after Sabbath, before their congregations? It is the mere dead carcase of Christianity. It is Christianity divested of its energy and its power. It is the merest mockery of human wretchedness. Is this an uncharitable announcement? Look at it and judge for yourselves. We look them once more in the face, and ask our brethren—Do you not say to the sinner that he is perfectly able to believe and to be saved? Do you not tell him that it would be unjust in God to condemn him, if he had not the power savingly to believe? Do you not assure him that he possesses "*all the powers required for considering, understanding, believing, choosing,* [?] *loving and hating, speaking and acting; and, moreover, for asking*"? But when the sinner comes to be wrought upon by such statements as these, so as to find himself most uneasy in the midst of his remaining unbelief, and would instantly flee to Jesus for safety, what do you not say to him?—in what way do you set the man's conscience at rest *for time,* and leave him waiting and waiting and waiting, under the conviction that it is his duty *to wait on, without the possession of perfect and solid peace with God?* You inform him that he *wants the power to will* to believe! You tell him, that when you spoke of ability, it was not *moral,* but only *natural* ability to which you referred; and by your misty metaphysical distinction, you cloud and obscure the poor man's soul—you hide from his eye the sun of righteousness, by this metaphysical mist which you throw around the sphere of his mental vision! To what does this vaunted distinction, after all, amount? Like every other distinction got up for the purpose of mere evasion, we have a *distinction without a difference.* We have the same thing presented before us under a different name. Under the title of "*moral inability,*" the sinner is informed that he has no power to believe; while, under the title, "*natural ability,*" the man is forthwith instructed that he possesses full power to believe; and that God himself could not justly punish him for unbelief, if he *could not* believe. Must we be charged with being *uncharitable,* because we call this a manifest contradiction? Is it uncharitable to speak the truth in love? We feel it to be painful, but we do not admit it to be uncharitable, to speak of that whereby esteemed brethren are themselves deceived, and whereby they most unintentionally deceive and ruin immortal souls, and to call it by its proper name. We use the words of the most *charitable* among living divines when we say to our fellow-sinners—"*This is all delusion—cheat not your souls with words—believe not those who would lay your consciences to sleep on the pillow of an imaginary inability.*"

The esteemed writer from whom these words are again quoted, immediately adds, "*Unwillingness is the word.*" Here is "*the word*" —What means this "*word*"? Dr. Wardlaw means by it *inability to will.* But while the doctor evidently refers to "beloved Ultra-Calvinistic brethren," against whose teaching he warns his fellow-sinners, when he says, "*believe not those who would lay your consciences to sleep on the pillow of an imaginary inability;*" and while we admit that there is ample room for the faithful warning, ought we not to say to the doctor—"*Physician heal thyself*"?

Does *he* not differ from those divines against whose pernicious doctrine he so faithfully warns men only *in words—mere words?* What is the alteration which the doctor proposes? It is the change of *a word!* "Unwillingness [says he] is *the word.*" The brethren against whose teaching Dr. Wardlaw lifts his faithful voice inculcate the notion of inability *to do.* Dr. Wardlaw himself inculcates the sinner's inability *to will to do.* No wonder that the same "Alliance," styled "Evangelical," can contain them both. They can shake hands over the *inability!* But we humbly submit that if this inability be, as this doctor says it is, in the one case "*imaginary,*" it is no less imaginary in both cases. Dr. Candlish very justly observes respecting it, somewhere in his attempts to combat Dr. Wardlaw's unanswerable arguments in favour of a universal atonement, that this is merely removing the inability into "a niche farther back." It is merely assigning to it a different position in the unbroken and indestructible *chain of necessity!* Call it natural, or call it moral, or call it by any fine name you choose—it is inability after all—"*an imaginary inability.*"

If we were, therefore, unhappily compelled to make our choice between two evils, we should choose the least, and adhere the rather to Dr. Candlish and "*those*" against whose pernicious teaching Dr. Wardlaw lifts his warning voice. We hesitate not to say to our *semi*-brethren—pernicious as the out-and-out orthodox teaching admittedly is, it is not by any means so pernicious as your own; and the reason is, that it is far more honest and consistent with itself, and far less truckling and deceptive, than is that half-and-half Calvinism which a miserable *expediency* has originated and patronized. Your system is a mere catch-penny system—it is no system at all. It wants the consistency even of error, and down it must speedily fall of its own accord. It has already slipped away out of the hands of all those who have preceded the Congregationalists and the "United Church" in their march out of Calvin-land, and it is our happiness to anticipate the time when it will be no longer expedient for the expediency brethren to retain it.

What is YOUR gospel, which you call it uncharitable to denounce as an imposition and a cheat? You go to the dungeon of the condemned man, and you tell him that you are the bearers of good news—"good tidings of great joy." You say to him that he has perfect freedom to enter the palace of his sovereign, and ask and obtain whatever he desires. And at this announcement the poor man's heart begins to leap for gladness. But you point him instantly to the bolts and bars and heavy chains which bind him to his prison-house, and you remind him that he has not the power to move, and you have no authority to set him free from the spot to which he is bound! And yet you say to him that he has the power to enter the palace, and you entreat him to enter, and you rebuke him because he is not found at the foot of the throne asking and obtaining whatever his heart desires!! Is not this the very essence of absurdity? Does it not amount to the most deliberate cruelty thus to insult and mock and tantalize the miserable and the unfortunate? WHY? Simply because *you know* that the poor man has not the power to move from his dungeon, and you admit he must first of all walk outside of that dungeon before it is possible for him to approach the palace of his sovereign. True, indeed, IF the poor man were once disengaged from his fetters and out of his prison-house, he has the power to walk up to the palace. And YOUR gospel depends upon this miserable "IF"!! The man has the power to take the second step, IF the first step were once accomplished! But the first step he has no power to take! Why, then, not deal HONESTLY with the poor man at once, and say plainly to him that you have NO GOSPEL to him at all?

But such is the sum and substance of the gospel which *you* have for sinners of the human race. It *sounds* at first like music from on high. It falls upon the ears of your hearers like sounds of sweetest melody. It is so free!—it is so full! It takes within its ample grasp the world—the whole world "without distinction and without exception!" But *examine it*—and what is there in it all for any sinner to cling to in the hour of need? Simply an assurance that the man is able to save himself *without the Holy Spirit!* Here is one side of your vaunted gospel, and looking at it in this, its most unlimited aspect, it amounts to a downright *falsehood.* But turn round the other side which embraces not the world, but takes in exclusively "the special few," and what does this "gospel" say? It assures men that they have no power to will—no power to take the first, the essential step back again to God—no power to will even to consider what the Holy Ghost says unto them—but that an iron chain of necessity binds their will down to the dark prison of their unbelief, until a special, direct, mystical, irresistible, and inexplicable influence shall, somehow or other, burst their fetters and set them free! Here, then, is the other aspect of what you call gospel, and looking at it in this "special reference" we find it to involve another *falsehood*, no less destructive than the former.

"Now, my fellow-sinners, this is all delusion." So truly has Dr. Wardlaw spoken of the system which has been examined in the first four of the Lectures, which we have been privileged to deliver in your hearing. We think we are warranted to apply the doctor's own expressive words to his own theology; and while we do so, we trust that while we condemn the system of this excellent writer no less strongly than he himself condemns the system of those whom he still loves as brethren, we shall not be awanting in cultivating towards him, and all from whom we differ, the same spirit of expansive charity. But we want more than mere *verbal* charity;—we want charity *in deed;* and we are therefore desirous that our brethren who are most industrious in circulating against us the slanderous charge of denying the necessity of the Holy Spirit's needful influence, would be so charitable as gird themselves to the task of *proving* what they gratuitously assert, and charitably pointing out to all men, if they can, from the Word of God, that the truth which we maintain involves the error which they are pleased calumniously to charge against it. We have ventured to show our brethren what we deem an example of charity, when we have not only asserted, but endeavoured at great length *to prove,* that the system which they themselves patronize involves a denial of the great truth for which all Christian men must ever be forward earnestly to contend.

We have most gratefully availed ourselves of the admissions which our brethren have made, as the result of Scripture examination and clear and solid proof which has not been, and cannot be, successfully met and overthrown. They have proved that Jesus died for all men, and that all men without exception are able to believe. This they have proved,—this we have admitted; and so far we have gratefully and joyfully accepted of their Scriptural and enlightened concessions. But when they come in with their "special influence," we ask them, how they reconcile this with what they have proved to be true in reference to every sinner's perfect ability to believe, and we are informed in reply, that the sinner is able to believe *without it.* We then ask, what they mean by this special influence. They inform us that they mean to describe thereby the influence which precedes the sinner's will, and must needs take the precedency of the sinner's will, before the sinner can believe—the influence of the Holy Ghost. Here it is that we pause and take leave to dispute with our brethren the truthfulness of their theory. We admit that the Holy Spirit's influence must needs precede the sinner's will before it is possible for the man either to will aright or to believe aright; but it is evident that this influence, whatever be its nature, cannot be "*special*" or exclusively restricted to the elect alone, unless it be true that the elect only are possessed of the ability to believe. But our brethren have proved that all men, without exception, are able to believe, and are therefore justly punishable for unbelief. We leave them therefore to take their choice between the denial of what they have proved to be true; or the denial of the necessity of the Holy Spirit in order to the production of faith; or the abandonment of their theory of election, whereby the influence of the Spirit is falsely imagined to be specially and exclusively confined to the elect. Our heart's desire and prayer for our brethren is, that they may speedily abandon this last-mentioned error, and come forth consistently in the strength of the Lord, to the acknowledgment of THE WHOLE TRUTH.

LECTURE EIGHTH.

ELECTION TO A SPECIAL INTEREST IN THE WORK OF THE SPIRIT—OPPOSED TO THE SCRIPTURE TESTIMONY RESPECTING THE NATURE OF DIVINE INFLUENCE—DIVINE DRAWING IDENTIFIED WITH DIVINE TEACHING—MAY BE RESISTED—"THE SPIRITS IN PRISON"—THE MURDERERS OF STEPHEN—THE THEORY OF A COMMON DIVINE INFLUENCE WHICH CANNOT SAVE—THE SPIRIT WORKS BY MEANS.

GEN. vi. 3.—"My Spirit shall not always strive with man."

ACTS vii. 57.—"Ye do always RESIST THE HOLY GHOST; as your fathers did, so do ye."

JOHN vi. 45.—"It is written in the prophets, And they shall be all taught of God. Every man, therefore, that hath heard and hath learned of the Father cometh unto me."

I WISH you, my friends, to examine the doctrine of election, which we are now considering, in the light of the Holy Scriptures, and, with that view, I have already directed your attention to several plain and simple texts, whose testimony no candid man can possibly overlook or disregard. And I now close the consideration of this important subject by inviting your attention to one other general remark. We object to this doctrine of election, because,

IV. It is opposed to the Scripture statements which point out to us the nature of the work of the Spirit.

The Word of God not only asserts the necessity of the Spirit's work—it speaks very plainly of the nature of that work in the conversion of the soul. It tells us precisely what is *the kind* of influence which the Spirit exerts upon the souls of men in order to bring them back to God. It is styled a "*drawing*" of the soul on the part of God; it is a *persuasive* influence, adapted by infinite wisdom, to the nature of the soul; it is not like that influence which is exerted upon inert and unconscious and unthinking matter; it is such influence as is adapted to the nature and properties of mind. It is not the turning of a mountain, but the revolution of a mind; not the dragging of a body, but the drawing of a soul, which this influence seeks to effect. And accordingly, we find the Sacred Scriptures representing the matter exactly in this light. We cannot conceive of a more direct or explicit statement upon this point than what is embodied in John vi. 45, wherein our Saviour himself very clearly intimates to his disciples the precise manner in which the Father draws. We have seen that, in the 44th verse, he asserts the absolute and indispensable necessity of the influence in order to enable any man to come to him—"No man *can come* to me, except the Father who hath sent me draw him."

But he immediately instructs us respecting the nature of this influence—he instantly informs us in what way the Father draws, when he adds, "It is written in the prophets, And they shall be all *taught* of God. Every man, therefore, that hath heard, and hath learned of the Father, cometh unto me." You will observe the precise phraseology which our Saviour uses, with the evident design of anticipating and correcting the blunders into which dreamy and mystifying theologians should be apt to fall. He does not use the expression "draweth" at all in the 45th verse. He uses the expressions, "taught of God," "heard and learned of the Father;" and observe, more particularly still, our Saviour uses these expressions in order to render it impossible for any man, without the most obvious perversion of his words, to affirm that the *drawing* is anything different from the *teaching*, or the *hearing* and *learning* of the Father, anything different from the soul's voluntary submission to the drawing influence of the Spirit. It is impossible for any man to come without the drawing influence; but all men are taught of God, and every man who hears and learns of this divine teacher, infallibly cometh unto Christ. Such is our Saviour's statement. Do you not see, therefore, that the *drawing* of the Spirit and the *teaching* of the Spirit are here identified? Is it not plain, from these words, that the Spirit draws by teaching, and that wherever the Spirit teaches there he draws, and that whosoever listens to his teaching, and learns at his feet, actually cometh unto Jesus? The persuasive influence of the Holy Spirit, whereby he draws men to Jesus and to happiness, is here strongly contrasted with the opposing influence of the Scribes and Pharisees, whereby the souls of the people were seduced away from Christ. And whereas those infatuated men and women who submitted to be taught by those erring teachers, and heard and learned at *their* feet, did not and could not come to Jesus, it was very different with those who regarded the teaching of God the Spirit rather than the fallible and erroneous teaching of fallible men; for while the former could not possibly come to Christ, every one of the latter "who hath heard and learned of the Father [Jesus emphatically declares] cometh unto me."

You see, therefore, how it is that the Spirit of God draws the human soul; it is by his own infallible teaching. And you see, farther, how it is that any soul is drawn by the Spirit; it is by disregarding the mere teaching of mere men, who would set up their own fallible creeds and confessions and catechisms and sermons, as if they were to be placed upon a level with the Word of God, thereby, like the ancient Pharisees, setting aside, by their traditions, the Scriptures of truth. It is by setting aside all such mere human authority—by disregarding all such fallible and priestly dictation to the conscience—by elevating the Word of God to its legitimate position of supremacy above all human creeds—by acting out practically the great principle of the Reformation, and practically asserting, in the face of an aspiring and ignorant clergy, the right and duty of private individual judgment as to the

Scriptures of truth—by every man remembering that it is not to his ministers or elders, but to his God, that he is responsible for his belief; or (to use the language of Jesus himself, in the verse we are now considering) it is by hearing and learning *of the Father*, as he speaks by the Spirit in the Bible, that men are drawn of God, and brought to Christ and to happiness.

But while such is the doctrine of the verse before us, that doctrine is denied and set aside, in order to make room for the strange notion of election we are now engaged in examining. You have already seen that, in order to bolster up this strange notion, its advocates find it necessary to maintain that sinners are quite able to believe, and do all their duty, without the influence of the Spirit; but, in connexion with this, they hold the theory of a special influence, which they inform us is directly and mysteriously exerted upon the minds of the elect, in order to make them willing to believe, and which is withheld from all the rest of the human race, who, if they were only willing, could be saved without it. This thing, then, which they call a special influence, is not the influence of the divine teaching. It is not the influence exerted upon the soul when the soul hears and learns of the Father. We are told that it is something else—something different from—something over and above that influence of which alone our Saviour speaks, in the 44th and 45th verses of the sixth chapter of John's gospel. We have demanded to know *what* it is, and *where* it is spoken of in the Word of God—and, strange to say, its supporters cannot tell! They cannot inform us what this special influence is! But what is still more strange, whenever we come to press them for proof of its existence, from the Word of God, they refer us to such passages as those we are now considering; but whenever we begin to examine these passages, we find that they inform us distinctly of the reality and necessity and distinctive nature of the Spirit's work. These texts inform us that the Spirit works *by means*—that he draws men to Jesus by presenting truth before their minds—that it is only when taught of God, and when they hear and learn of the Father, they ever come to Christ. But this is the very thing which these electionists deny. They deny the doctrine so plainly stated in the very passages of Scripture which are most frequently upon their lips! And it is because they deny what we submit to you Christ plainly says, about the nature of divine drawing—(when he exhibits it not as direct or without means, but as exerted by means of teaching or instruction, and when he thereby exhibits it, not as physical but moral in its nature),—that we hold their doctrine to amount to a mere figment of the human imagination.

But I here call your attention to a somewhat more tangible feature of this dreamy and mystical theology. We are informed by its supporters, that this special influence whereby the work of the Spirit is set aside, is altogether *irresistible*. We are not informed what it is, although we are told that it is not divine *teaching*. But when we come to inquire a little more closely into the matter, we are told that whatever it be, it cannot be resisted by any sinner on whose mind it is once exerted. This additional piece of information seems to us quite decisive, in order to stamp this special influence as a mere delusion. It cannot be the influence of *the Holy Ghost*—whatever men may choose to call it. And the reason why we speak so decidedly here, is, that the Bible speaks decidedly upon this particular point. And here, my friends, you will find some use for the passages of Scripture which, in the outset, I have requested you to mark. We are informed by its friends that *their* "special influence" cannot be resisted, and that it is never exerted upon the minds of any of those sinners who perish in their unbelief. Well, then, we take our brethren at their word, and we say to them—Brethren, that influence of which you speak *cannot* therefore be the influence to which *God himself refers*, when he says, in Genesis vi. 3, "My Spirit shall not always strive with man," for *there* was an influence which was *resisted*, and *overcome* by the antediluvian transgressors, who, because of their obstinacy and sin, were ultimately swept away by the waters of the deluge. The simple question here is — did these antediluvian transgressors resist the influence of the Holy Spirit or did they not? That these men resisted a very powerful influence when they resisted the preaching of Noah, our brethren are ready to admit, but they deny that it was the influence of the Spirit which was resisted; for if they did not deny this, they would need to give up their system of theology which is based upon the theory of election, whereby they are taught, that the Spirit of God cannot possibly be resisted by any with whom he strives. But I stand before you this evening pledged to demonstrate the utter falsehood of that theory of election, and the consequent delusiveness of that system of theology which is based upon it. And here is one of my proofs—*God himself* gives us to understand that *his Spirit* strove with the antediluvian sinners who finally perished. And have we not a right to ask any man who says that God's Spirit did not strive with these men (otherwise they would have all been saved), —"Who art thou, O man, that repliest against God?" How comes it to pass that proud and vain mortals persist in setting up their own imaginations in direct opposition to the most obvious truths of God's own Word? It is all for the purpose of upholding an unscriptural and soul-destroying system of theology, which teaches sinners to believe, that if the spirit of God only strive with them they cannot possibly be lost, and which thereby instructs them to stifle their consciences, and remain at ease under the garb of a dry and fruitless attendance on the means of grace, while they say to their souls—"Soul, take thine ease and be at peace, for if the Spirit of God only strive with thee, thou canst not possibly be lost." Now, my friends, I hesitate not to make my appeal to your own consciences this night, while I direct you to this simple statement, "My Spirit shall not always strive with man," and just as if I were proposing a question to any class of Sabbath-school children, do I ask every one of you to say, what the doctrine of this passage is,—Does it not contain the doctrine that the Spirit of God did strive with the generation of men who existed before the flood? It was not the means of grace *merely* that these men resisted; it was the influence of the Spirit, exerted through the instrumentality of the means. I charge you, therefore, this evening, to listen to God's Word; and to reject the traditions of men which contradict that Word, and would lead you to believe that the influence of the Spirit was not exerted upon those men whose spirits are now shut up in the prison-house of despair. Permit me here to refer you to another inspired condemnation of that doctrine of election which is founded upon the error of a special influence. The passage is one which bears directly upon the statement from Genesis which we have now before us. It is written in 1 Peter iii. 18–20: "For Christ also hath once suffered for sins, the just for the unjust, that he might bring us to God; being put to death in the flesh, but quickened by the Spirit. By which also he went and preached unto the spirits in prison; which sometime were disobedient, when once the long-suffering of God waited in the days of Noah, while the ark was a preparing, wherein few, that is, eight souls, were saved by water." Now, here you notice, (1,) That Christ preached to the spirits in the prison-house of despair. (2,) That the time when Christ preached to those lost and imprisoned spirits was in the days of Noah—while yet these spirits now in prison were inhabiting their fleshy and mortal tabernacles,—before they were swept into prison by the waters of the flood, and while yet the long-suffering of God waited for their repentance. (3,) You will observe more particularly, that it was by the putting forth of the influence of his Spirit upon them, through means of preaching—the preaching of Noah, the preacher of righteousness (as we are elsewhere informed)—it was by his own Spirit *thus* striving with them, in order to bring them to repentance, that Christ did most earnestly seek to prevent those spirits from going down into the prison of everlasting woe. Now, can any honest and candid man look such facts—divinely recorded facts—as these are, fairly in the face, and at the same time affirm, that the influence of the Spirit cannot possibly be resisted? I have no doubt, my dear friends, that you see clearly enough the bearing of this question upon the great doctrinal point now under discussion. You see that if this question be honestly answered as God himself answers it, the entire doctrine of election in the faith of which, you, and I, and thousands more, were unhappily nursed up from our infancy, falls to the ground—a baseless and demolished thing. But if your eye does not see farther than this, you will fail to appreciate the infinite importance of the question which I am so earnestly pressing upon your notice. My fellow-sinners, your own souls, and the souls of your children, and the souls of your friends, and the souls of the thousands and tens of thousands who even now are posting onwards and downwards to the doleful prison-house, are *practically interested*, and will be eternally affected, either for weal or for woe, by the question which I now press upon your notice! Does God himself not declare that his good Spirit strove, and strove long, and strove earnestly, with those lost spirits which are now in prison, enduring the dreadful penalties of their stubborn and unnatural resistance? The teachers to whom ye trust, with united voice tell you, "No," for our *Confession of Faith* says, that the influence of the Spirit cannot be resisted! Here, then, is a dreadful controversy! It is a controversy between the infallible God and fallible men! Men and brethren, on whose side are ye resolved to stand? Will ye idolize men because these men are called ministers of Christ? Will ye stand out striving with your Maker, and confronting the truth of God by a blasphemous contradiction, and stay your souls any longer upon a mere arm of flesh? Can you forget that it is thus written, "*Cursed be the man who putteth his trust in man*"? I appeal, therefore, this night, from the verdict of the men who teach you, to the infallible verdict of the living God—the God of truth, who cannot possibly lie and who cannot possibly be mistaken; and in opposition to Scotland's vaunted theology—whereby the people of my native land have been too long deceived and deluded, and, in too many instances, eternally ruined—do I this night declare, that there is not a soul among you all with whom the Spirit does not earnestly strive; and that if any of you perish, your blood is on your own heads, and ye shall go down into despair *resisting the influence of the Holy*

Spirit, whereby every soul of you may happily be saved!

But this leads me to call up before you another infallible witness in support of the position I am now seeking to maintain,—it is the testimony of *the Spirit himself,* speaking through the lips of a dying martyred saint, to which I now summon your attention. You find it written down in Acts vii. 21: "Ye do always *resist the Holy Ghost:* as your fathers did, so do ye." In the face of this evidence, we are very coolly informed, by our modern theologians, that the Holy Ghost cannot be resisted! Well, then, my fellow-men, it is not for me to dictate, but it is for you, as in the sight of God, to make your choice. Which will ye believe? Choose ye between the Word of God and the traditions of fallible men, and say which ye will believe! Do you ask me to inform you how it is possible for them to meet such evidence as this, and yet retain their soul-destroying doctrines? You may well propose the question, and I shall now try, as briefly as I can, to answer it. This evidence splits them up into two parties, who each endeavour vainly to assail it from two very different points. One party says—"These men did not resist the Holy Ghost at all—it was only the preaching of the apostles, and the miraculous evidence by which it was proved to be divine, that the men resisted." Another party rejoins—"It was not the proper influence—the special influence—the only influence which converts the soul, that these men resisted—for *this* we hold it to be impossible for any man to resist—they resisted the *common influence* of the Spirit, which is not, properly speaking, the influence of the Spirit at all, since it never did, and never can, convert a single soul to God." Such is the double battery which Calvinists have erected, in order to assail this impregnable fortress of the truth of God, and thereby, if possible, save from destruction their "horrible decree." But most evident it is, that both parties fail so much as to touch the real point of assault. That point is involved and exhibited in the very distinct assertion of the Word of God, wherein we are plainly informed, that the murderers of Stephen were going down to hell resisting, in their downward progress, the true and proper influence of the Holy Ghost, which was drawing and inviting them upwards to heaven: they were posting onwards to destruction in spite of all the efforts of the Holy Ghost to save them. Now, it will not do for one set of Calvinists to tell us that these infatuated men did not resist the Holy Ghost at all, but that they simply resisted the means of grace, which in themselves can never save a single soul. We admit that they resisted the means of grace, but we maintain that they resisted *more than the means*, for we are distinctly informed that they resisted *the Holy Ghost* himself.

Do you not observe the recklessness with which those assailants assault the Scriptures of truth? In a former Lecture, we quoted to you a passage from one of their books, wherein they endeavour to prove that any sinner who chooses, may be saved without the Holy Ghost altogether. You will remember that the writer quoted the verse wherein Paul says to Timothy, that from a child he had known the Holy Scriptures, which are able to make men wise unto salvation; and because Paul does not mention the name of the Holy Ghost in that particular connexion, it was maintained by this writer, that Paul inculcates the doctrine that any sinner who chooses may easily become wise unto salvation, without the influence of the Spirit. Now, here is a passage where the Holy Ghost is expressly named, and where not one word is said about the Scriptures and the means of grace; and what do those reckless perverters of God's word *now* do? They reverse their own system of interpretation altogether, by overlooking the distinct mention that is here made of 'the Holy Spirit, and insisting that this Scripture passage does not refer to the Spirit at all, but only to the means of grace! In speaking of one passage where the Scriptures *are* mentioned, but where the Spirit *is not* named, they insist that no reference whatever is made, even by implication, to the Spirit. And this they do in order to bolster up their doctrine, that the Spirit is not needed to enable any sinner to be saved! But when you take them to another passage, where the Holy Ghost *is* expressly named and where the means of grace *are not* mentioned, they exactly reverse their former principle of interpretation, and insist, that though the Holy Ghost *is named,* he is not at all referred to in the text; and though the Scriptures are *not named,* they, along with the other means of grace, are exclusively referred to! And this they do for the same reason as before—they must at all hazards uphold their system of theology, and hold by a special, irresistible influence, in order to keep up their theory of election, and avert its threatened destruction! *The truth of God* needs to be defended by no such unseemly weapons. We have mentioned to you before, that where the Scriptures, or other means of grace are mentioned, the Holy Spirit is not thereby excluded. And so, when it is said—"The Scriptures are able to make men wise unto salvation," it is not implied that the Scriptures are able to do this without the influence of the Spirit. And so here, when it is said to men who perished—"Ye do always resist the Holy Ghost," the Scriptures and other means of grace are not excluded, and it is not implied that these murderers did not resist the means; but what we affirm is, they resisted more than the means—they resisted the influence of the Holy Ghost himself—that very influence whereby the Spirit saves the soul.

I submit, therefore, to your unprejudiced and honest judgments, whether it be not unanswerably proved, by the text before you, that the Holy Ghost has been resisted, and may therefore again be resisted, by the sinners with whom he strives. But what do we make of the other mode of interpretation whereby the force of the passage is sometimes evaded? We are told that it is the *common* influence of the Spirit which is here said to be resisted; and when we ask what is the meaning of the expression, a common influence, we are informed that it is an influence whereby God does not mean to save, and which cannot save the soul. This is what we are told. But the all-important question is, BY WHOM are we told this?—to whom are we indebted for this marvellous piece of information, about an influence of the Spirit which cannot possibly save any sinner's soul? and on whose authority are we called upon to believe in it? This will not be said to be an unreasonable demand. Let us see one solitary passage in the whole Bible which speaks of an influence of the Holy Ghost which *needs to be supplemented* by another kind of Divine influence, in order to become adequate to the salvation of the soul, and we shall instantly believe. But of all the absurdities of error, this is the most absurd! Of all the weak positions which erring men are compelled to occupy, this is the most weak and infantile. And hence it is, that even among Modern Calvinists, it is only "*the weaker brethren*" who are found to skulk into this most unscriptural position. Every reader of his Bible knows well, that there are not *two kinds* of ordinary Divine influence spoken of throughout its pages. There is not a work of the Holy Ghost for all men, and another work or influence of a different kind for the elect only, spoken of in the Scriptures. There are, indeed, *miraculous gifts*, and *gifts of inspiration* referred to; but *these* are not surely included in what is called the common influence, which all men are said, by this hypothesis, to possess, though it never can save a single soul; and *these* are not included by our brethren in the thing which they call a special influence, which they say is irresistible. And there are different *degrees* of Divine influence referred to in the Bible—one man possessing comparatively less of the Spirit than another, and all being commanded to be "filled with the Spirit." But we challenge any man to adduce one single passage of Scripture which so much as hints at two separate and distinct *kinds* of influence—the one common to all men, but which cannot save, and never did save a single soul—the other confined exclusively to the elect, but which, from its very nature, cannot possibly be resisted. The truth is, that as there is one God and Father of all, and one Lord and Saviour of all, even so there is but one Spirit who strives with all, and who saves and sanctifies all those who believe. And as there is one Spirit, so there is but one *kind* of spiritual influence, which is common to all men, and which, when any man resists, he resists *the Holy Ghost.* Neither are we left in ignorance as to the *nature* of this influence, for it is said in the text we are now considering, " Ye do always resist the Holy Ghost: *as your fathers did*, so do ye." Now, that it is resistible by men, is obvious at the very first reading of the verse. But when the question is put, *How* does the Spirit exert his influence?—is it *directly* upon the soul, or *by means*, and through the instrumentality of truth? we have only to betake ourselves, not to the dreams and speculations of fallible men, far less to the musty creeds of men who most religiously murdered their fellow creatures, on the charge of witchcraft!—" we have a more sure word of prophecy, to which we would do well to take heed." The text refers us to the fact, that as their fathers resisted the Holy Ghost, so did they. Now the question is—Does the word of God supply us with information as to the way in which their fathers resisted the Spirit? It does. Turn with me, therefore, for example, to the ninth chapter of the book of Nehemiah, verses 20th and 30th: "Thou gavest also *thy good Spirit* to instruct them, and withheldest not thy manna from their mouth, and gavest them water for their thirst." And again (ver. 30), "Yet many years didst thou forbear them, and testifiedest against them *by the Spirit in thy prophets;* yet would they not give ear." Thus was it that the fathers of Stephen's murderers resisted the Holy Ghost; and thus did these their children resist the Holy Ghost; and thus does every sinner on the face of the earth resist the Holy Ghost, who refuses to believe the testimony of the Spirit, speaking through means of the Scriptures, and to enter into the possession of eternal life. It is thus *by means* that God the Father draws the sinner to himself; and it is only when the sinner hears and learns of the Father, speaking to all men by his Spirit through the Word, that he cometh unto Jesus, and finds rest unto his weary soul.*

And now, my friends, I have done with this unscriptural theory of election, the falsehood of which I have endeavoured, in the four last Lectures, to establish. We

* See the very able Treatise upon the Work of the Spirit, by T. W. Jenkyn, D. D., of London.

shall very speedily, if God spare us together, come to set before you a theory of election from the Word of God which excludes none of you from salvation, but which is gloriously consistent with the gospel message which comes to every sinner on the face of the earth. We have said that we shall do this, if God shall be pleased to spare us together. But, beloved friends, there is much in that little word "IF." It may be that we shall not all meet again beneath the sun—it may be, that we shall not all meet until we shall face each other before the judgment-seat of Christ. My friends, God is my witness when I assure you, that the glorious truth which I am feebly endeavouring to set before you, gives MY sinful and guilty and hell-deserving soul glorious hope in the prospect of that day. I tell you more, when I assure you, that I too once preached the very error which I have been endeavouring to expose, and against which, to my dying hour, and with my latest breath, I would warn my fellow-men. That doctrine never gave me peace in the prospect of meeting with my God. It never assured even the preacher himself, that he was one of the elect. The preacher knew he was "the chief of sinners;" but how could he know that he was one of the special favourites of God without a special revelation, which to him was never once vouchsafed? My dear friends—may I not add, my fellow-sinners—sinners against God as well as he who now speaks to you —are *ye* possessed of another revelation different from that which lies before me? Have *your teachers* furnished you with a Bible to the elect? Have you got from them a message which will serve you in the face of death, judgment, and eternity, if their doctrine of election be not all a fable? If God has indeed brought only some among you into existence under the possibility of being saved, is it possible for you to know which of you is interested in the love of God, so as to cherish good hope beyond the grave? It is impossible! But I have proved to you that the current doctrine of election is a falsehood and a lie; therefore, I say, it is not impossible for you this very evening to come to peace with God through the knowledge of his love—his matchless love to you as well as to me. There is no Divine influence kept back from you. No. "He that spared not his own Son, but gave him up to the death for you all, shall he not with him also freely give you all things?" Think you, then, that when he gave his Son, he will withhold the needful influence of his Spirit? Think you that he will hold you guilty for not believing, and yet keep back the one thing needful to enable you to believe? No, brethren. You have something to believe, and that something is true; and that something is not bad news, but good tidings of great joy to every one of you, in the solemn prospect of "THAT DAY," till which, I have said, we may never all meet again. But what is that something which you are bound to believe, and which, if you do not believe, you make the God of truth a liar to his face? Tell me, my beloved friends, what you would like it to be? In the face of death and judgment, what, my fellow-sinner, would be good news to thy sinful soul? Riches? Honours? No! no! These will not comfort thee at the hour of death! What if, at that solemn hour, an angel from on high were to descend and sing—"Fear not: for unto *thee* was born *a Saviour!* and that Saviour bare thy sins in his own body on the tree! and that Saviour hath sent me down to assure *thee*, sinner, of his love; and, through his blood, to proclaim to *thee* the pardon of thy sins!" You say—"Give me an *angel's* word and then I will believe, and will not fear to face my God." My fellow-sinner, I point thee to *more than an angel's word!* I point thee away from the errors of men to the Word of *the Holy Spirit.* In that Word there is truth—in that Word there is power, the power of God unto salvation to every one that believeth. That Word is the word of the gospel, with which the Spirit approaches thy sinful soul, and says that Jesus loved *thee!* and shed his blood for *thee!* and that pardon through that blood is proclaimed to *thee!* Such is the testimony of the Spirit to every sinner in this house to-night—such is the good tidings of great joy which, not an angel, but God himself addresses to you all! O then, friends, believe Him even now, and yield to his truth even now, for, "Behold, now is the accepted time; behold, now is the day of salvation."

LECTURE NINTH.

THE BIBLE DOCTRINE OF ELECTION—ELECTION, THE ACT OF SEPARATION—SEPARATION FROM THE WORLD—SEPARATION BY GOD—ULTIMATE AND SUBORDINATE OBJECTS OF ELECTION—DISTINCTIVE NATURE OF ELECTION—SEPARATION THROUGH MEANS—"MAKE YOUR CALLING AND ELECTION SURE"—IMPORTANCE OF HOLINESS.

EPHES. i. 4.—"According as he hath chosen us in him before the foundation of the world, that we should be holy and without blame before him in love."

2 THESS. ii. 13.—"But we are bound to give thanks alway to God for you, brethren beloved of the Lord, because God hath from the beginning chosen you to salvation through sanctification of the Spirit, and belief of the truth."

1 PETER i. 2.—"Elect according to the foreknowledge of God the Father, through sanctification of the Spirit, unto obedience and sprinkling of the blood of Jesus Christ."

2 PETER i. 10.—"Wherefore the rather, brethren, give diligence to make your calling and election sure; for if ye do these things, ye shall never fall."

THE question which falls now to be considered, is one of engrossing interest. It is a question which lies at the foundation of all theology, and which is indissolubly connected with the eternal destinies of every soul of the human race. WHAT IS ELECTION? (1,) What is the true and proper import of the term? (2,) What is the actual state of things which is necessarily and really presupposed by the electing process? (3,) Who is the sole and exclusive agent by whom the process of election is conducted? (4,) What is the grand ultimate end which God has in view, and what the proximate or subordinate objects which God in election proposes to accomplish? These are four preliminary questions which we wish you this evening to answer preparatory to the great fundamental question—WHAT IS ELECTION? And the solution of each and all of these subordinate points will open up the way for a brief exposition of a doctrine which, to this hour, has not met with that attention, nor occupied that position in the minds of men, which is everywhere assigned to it in the Word of God.

I. WHAT THEN IS THE IMPORT OF THE WORD?

It denotes the act, or process of separation, when one object is selected or set apart from other surrounding objects. Observe what we say. It is the act, or process of selection or separation. This is a remark so very plain and simple, that you are very apt to pass it over and to dismiss it from your minds by a mere cursory glance. But you will see the error of such conduct, when I inform you, that this remark, simple and plain and self-evident as it is, lies at the very foundation of the subject we are now seeking to expound to you. The truth is, that all error is the result of overlooking the most obvious facts. Men suppose that such things are so plain that they cannot possibly be denied, and it is here that the deceiver of souls gets advantage over his votaries. He gets them to forget altogether the plainest axioms. He leads them astray from truth, and astray from God, and astray from everlasting happiness, by making them careless about first principles, which are so obvious and so simple, that even a child may easily apprehend them. The idea of ELECTION is familiar to the mind of the youngest child who practically exemplifies every day its preference of one thing and its aversion to another. The very infant upon the breast knows practically what election is. Let it be surrounded by a number of strange faces, all seeking to engage its attention and to win its preference, and the child will turn away from them all, and hide its little face in the bosom of its mother. The little one chooses or selects, or sets apart for itself, the object to which it instinctively turns from among all the other objects which are set before it. There you see an illustration of the great principle involved in election. The events of every-day life are pregnant with examples. You want a servant to do your work, and many there are who are desirous to serve you; but you select one out of the many, and the act of separation, whereby you choose and separate one from among all the other applicants, is your deed of election. You want a man to represent you in the great council of the nation, and many there are who solicit your vote; but you fix upon one out of the many, and when the day and hour of election comes you hasten to the polling booth, and you practically exemplify the true and proper import of the term election. You separate the man for whom you vote from all the other claimants for your suffrage, and the act of separation is the act of election. The word has the same meaning to whatever subject it may happen to be wedded, and by whomsoever the right or privilege of election may happen to be exercised. It bears the same meaning in the Bible which is attached to it in the ordinary affairs of men. It implies the right to choose or to select, and it expresses in every instance the act or process of selection.

You cannot fail to notice the important difference between the purpose to select, and the act or process of election. The one exists when you have made up your minds how you are to act; the other has no existence, and cannot possibly have any existence, until the time when you come to carry your purpose into execution. Till then there is not, in point of fact, any election. You may speak indeed improperly and loosely, and you may say at the moment your mind is made up how you mean to act, that very moment the election, so far as you are concerned, is virtually decided. But, even when you do thus express yourselves, you do not mean to intimate that the electing process is already past. It is not the act or process of separation, but the purpose or decision of your mind, which, strictly and properly speaking, is the thing referred to when you say, that the election, so far as you are concerned, is decided whenever your mind is made up. In this case it is not election in fact, but election in purpose of which you speak. It is not THE ACT of selection or separation, but THE PURPOSE to elect which is indicated by your words. I have said that this distinction is important, and I now add, that it is a distinction which is paramount in importance. It is so very important, that if you fail to appreciate it and fully to understand it, you disqualify yourselves, in the very outset, for apprehending the great Bible doctrine of election altogether. But surely it is not difficult to understand this simple and important distinction. When a man has made up his mind to do anything whatever, every man can see clearly the difference between this, and the actual performance or execution of the purpose which has thus been formed. Now, it is universally admitted, that the term election means strictly and properly the actual process of separation. But it is universally forgotten that there is a very material difference between the purpose to elect or separate, and the actual process itself; which process alone is strictly and properly expressed by the term election. Take an example of election from the Word of God—the election of Aaron to the office of the priesthood. We know that Aaron was in the purpose of God elected from eternity to fill the sacerdotal office; but when we speak of election from eternity, we refer not to the election properly speaking, but to the purpose of God to separate the house of Levi from all the other tribes of Israel, in order to minister at the altar. We prove to you, from God's own words, that Aaron was not, in point of fact, elected by him to fill the sacerdotal office, until after the earth had opened her mouth and had swallowed up Korah, Dathan, and Abiram, before the eyes of the affrighted multitude, and until after the rod of Aaron "budded and brought forth buds, and bloomed blossoms, and yielded almonds" within the tabernacle of the Lord. You have read the seventeenth chapter of the book of Numbers, where God says to Moses :—(ver. 5,) "And it shall come to pass, that the man's rod, whom I SHALL choose, shall blossom." Here then is an example of election on the part of God, and God himself speaks of it not as a past or present, but as a future act. The election of Aaron, on the part of God, did not take place until Aaron was ACTUALLY SET APART to fill the sacerdotal office. In accordance with this example of election, you will understand the strict and proper import of the word. Properly understood, it means, and can mean nothing less and nothing else, than the actual process or deed of separation; and when it is spoken of as eternal, the reference is not to election properly so called, but to election in purpose, which is not the election itself, but the purpose to elect. There are many elections spoken of in the Scriptures of truth. There is *angelical* election, for we read of "elect angels;" there is a *national* election, for we read of the election of the Jewish nation, who were separated by God from all the surrounding nations as his peculiar people; there is, as we have seen, a *sacerdotal* election, as in the case of Aaron and the sons of Levi to the priestly office; there is a *regal* election, as in the separation of Saul, and after him of David the son of Jesse, to wield the sceptre and sit upon the throne and wear the crown; there is a *mediatorial* election, for Jesus the Son of God was styled "mine elect, in whom my soul delighteth," and separated or set aside from all the beings in the universe to stand between an offended God and a rebel world; and there is *evangelical* election, which consists in the separation of all who believe the gospel from the world around them, and such is that election of which we now speak.

Now what we wish you to notice is, that in all election, whether angelical or national or sacerdotal or regal or mediatorial or evangelical, there is the uniform development of the grand fundamental principle to which we now specially and particularly refer. In every instance, the election is nothing more and nothing less and nothing else than the act or process of separation itself, as distinguished from the purpose so to separate, or choose, or pick out, or select. The purpose is one thing, the election is another and separate thing altogether. The purpose is something in the mind of God; the election is the actual separation, which has no actual existence, and cannot possibly have any actual existence, until the purpose comes to be developed and carried into execution.

II. Our second inquiry now relates to the actual state of things presupposed by the very existence of election.

The very idea of angelical election presupposes the existence of other angels from whom the elect angels were separated; and so there could be no such thing as national election, if there had not existed at the period of separation other nations from whom the peculiar people were picked out and set aside. And it would be absurd to speak of an election or choosing of one man and his tribe to the priestly office, without at the same time assuming the existence of other men and other tribes, from among whom the chosen one was separated and set apart. And so, to come at once to the election of which we speak, it would be absurd in the extreme to speak of an actual selection or separation of believing men and women, without supposing the actual existence of a mass of unbelieving persons, from among whom the elect are separated. Is it not manifest at a single glance, that the act or process of separation, implies not only the actual existence of the persons who are separated, or elected, or chosen, but the equally actual existence of the very individual persons from among whom the elect are so separated and chosen? Is it not a monstrous absurdity to speak of AN ACTUAL selection and separation of a multitude of *nonentities* from among a host of other similar *nonentities?* It is not thus that the Bible instructs us, and it is not over a universe of mere ideas that Jehovah reigns. There was once an ideal philosophy which has been happily exploded and put to flight by a strong appeal to the common sense and the every-day apprehensions of mankind; and we still live under the reign of an IDEAL THEOLOGY which is already beginning to totter toward its downfall before the common sense of men who are content to make their appeal to, and draw their religion from, the infallible Word of the infallible God. It is not from among a generation of phantoms that the selection of which we speak is made. Jesus said unto some of the separated ones, "*I have chosen you out of the world.*" It was not out of an ideal world, but out of an existing world—a sinful, Saviour-crucifying and gospel-hating and salvation-despising world, that the elect were actually taken and set apart for God. You cannot suppose the act of separation as eternal save in the sense in which you can suppose the world itself to have existed from eternity. It existed from eternity in the mind and purpose of God. God purposed from eternity to create it. In like manner as you may figuratively and with an exclusive reference to the purpose, speak of the world existing from eternity, even so is it figuratively, and with a reference solely to purpose, said, that they who are united by faith to Christ are in him chosen from eternity. But it is evident to common sense itself, that the actual election or separation of some from the world—the act or process of choosing or picking them out of the world—necessarily presupposes the actual existence, not only of the elect themselves, but also of that identical world out of which they were literally chosen and actually separated for glory.

III. Our third question relates to the agent by whom the act of selection is carried into execution.

And here we need not pause nor hesitate even for a

moment—it is God alone who elects. But for this, there would be no election—no separation from the world at all. Did God not graciously choose us, we never could, and never would have been chosen. Here is the grace and here the glory of election. It is primarily and exclusively the doing of the Lord, and it is wondrous in our eyes. It is to the praise of the glory of his grace that there are any brands plucked from the burning—it is to the praise of the glory of his grace that there are any sinners united to the Saviour—it is to the praise of the glory of his grace that there are any souls saved from the pit of destruction, and welcomed among the angels of heaven to the regions of immortal blessedness. "Not unto us, O Lord, not unto us, but unto thy name be all the glory, for thy mercy and thy truth's sake."

IV. Our fourth inquiry relates to the grand ultimate end which God has in view in election, in connexion with the proximate or subordinate objects subserved thereby.

And here be it observed, that the grand ultimate end which God proposes here, and in everything that he does, is *his own glory*. God cannot possibly act save for this one grand ultimate object. He would cease to be God were he to propose to himself any other end than this. This is the highest, the noblest, the most worthy of all possible ends. This, therefore, is the only ultimate object and design worthy of a being of infinite excellence. The very same reason which would, and does render it sinful in any creature to propose to himself his own gratification or glory as the grand aim of all his doings, renders it impossible for God to propose to himself any other end. The creature is finite and dependent and imperfect and fallible; the Creator alone is infinite, independent, and infallible. He alone is infinite in every conceivable perfection; and he only is necessarily and legitimately the ultimate end and origin of all that can be called great or good or wise or holy in the wide universe.

But while the glory of God is the grand ultimate object which he has proposed to himself in election and in all that he does, there are certain subordinate and proximate ends which he proposes to effect in the separation of believers from the world. These proximate and subordinate ends are TWO. The one refers to the *state*, the other to the *character* of those who are the subjects of the separating or electing process. In reference to their *state*, the object which God has in view in their election or separation from the world is, their being placed in a position wherein they may enjoy daily and hourly access to the blood of Christ, and have their consciences sprinkled therewith from their daily and hourly shortcomings. In reference to their *character*, it is the design of God in their election to lead them on in a course of holy and progressive obedience, and ultimately to bring them forth perfect and without blame before him. Such are the two subordinate objects which God has in view in the separation or selection of sinners out of the world,—the one referring to their *state*, so that they may be partakers of all possible blessedness which they are capable of enjoying; and the other referring to their *character;* so that, reflecting the image of God, they may be capable to perform those high and exalted duties, and be made meet for those high and holy exercises in which it is at once their duty and their privilege to engage. We are not left to hesitate or debate for one moment as to these two objects being the secondary and proximate objects which God has in view in election. As to the first, we are informed in 1 Peter i. 2, that we are "elect *unto the sprinkling* of the blood of Christ." Here, then, is the most distinct intimation of the state of privilege into which God does in point of fact introduce believers by election. It is unto the daily sprinkling of the blood of Christ. So, then, just as they need pardon every day, they have freedom of access every day by faith into the holiest, having their consciences daily sprinkled with the blood of the atonement. And their state of blessedness is not referred to merely by the Apostle Peter, for Paul adds his testimony to the same effect, in witnessing upon this point. In 2 Thessalonians ii. 13, he reminds believers of the state of exalted blessedness to which they were chosen, saying, "God hath from the beginning chosen you *to salvation.*" Such is the state of blessedness, of present and future blessedness, which it is one design and object of God to confer by election. To this state all who believe are separated. To the enjoyment of the daily sprinkling, and the blessed hope of the glorious kingdom—to the present and everlasting enjoyment of all that is contained in that wondrous word, "SALVATION"—are they separated by God in the process of election.

But the second proximate object which God has in view, subordinate to his own glory, refers to the characters of those who are chosen. They are accordingly said by Peter, in the passage before referred to, to be elect "*unto obedience,*" as well as unto the daily sprinkling of the blood of Christ; and Paul says, in Ephesians i. 4, that they are chosen in order that they "should be holy and without blame before him in love." Here, then, is the second subordinate object of election clearly and distinctly and incontrovertibly announced. It is progressively holy obedience here and perfection hereafter, so that we may be without blame presented to the Father—without spot, or wrinkle, or any such thing. The king's daughter is thus to be adorned *without* in a robe of finest needle-work, being clothed in the righteousness of Christ himself; and she is to be all glorious *within* when, freed from every imperfection which cleaves to her here below, she shall meet her descending Lord in the clouds, and so be for ever with him in glory. Such is the twofold object which God, in election, proposes to accomplish, and does, in every instance, most graciously accomplish; and these two objects are not, in any case, inconsistent with his glory. By them his own glory will be most efficiently promoted and most worthily advanced.

We now come to the main inquiry, What is the specific or distinctive nature of Election? What is it which God does when he elects, or chooses, or separates believers from the world? The twofold object which God has in view in separating believers from the world cannot be mistaken, and will not here be overlooked. Permit me, therefore, to propose to you the simple question, What is it which, in any case, stands out as the *hindrance* towards the effecting of these two subordinate objects whereby, in every instance, the glory of God is most effectually advanced? This is the great problem to be solved; for it cannot be doubted that God is, in no case, uninterested or careless in reference to the advancement of his own glory. If you do not doubt this (and it is impossible for any man to doubt or question it for an instant), you will surely admit that God cannot possibly remain uninterested or careless in reference to the salvation of any sinner by whose salvation his glory would undoubtedly be advanced. If His glory would be advanced by one sinner being separated or elected out of the world, and set apart to the daily sprinkling of the blood of Christ, and to obedience, it follows, as a necessary consequence, that his glory would be much more illustriously manifested by every sinner on the face of the earth being so separated to the enjoyment of daily sprinkling and the following of all holiness. It is on this ground chiefly that there is joy among the angels over every sinner who repenteth. Where, then, lies the hindrance, in any instance, to the advancement of God's glory by the accomplishment of this twofold object of election? What is the hindrance, in the first place, to any sinner's enjoyment of the daily sprinkling of the blood of Christ? It lies in the state of condemnation in which, by his unbelief, the man is placed. And where, again, lies the hindrance to any sinner's voluntary obedience to God's commandments? It lies in that unregenerated heart and nature in which, by his unbelief, the man voluntarily remains. Here, then, is the twofold hindrance whereby the twofold object which God has in view in election is alone prevented. This is the only hindrance which prevents the separation of any, and every sinner, on the face of the earth, to the enjoyment of present and eternal happiness. Do you ask me then to say what is the distinctive nature of election? My reply is, election consists in the removal of this twofold hindrance. It does not consist in the removal of the condemnation *alone*—that is an act of God which is called by the name of justification;—it does not consist in the removal of the enmity of the unregenerated soul *alone*—that, too, is an act of God, and it is called by the name of regeneration;—but let the two be looked at in their combined state—look at the removal of the condemnation from the sinner's soul in connexion with the removal of the enmity from the sinner's heart, and you have a distinct idea of that process of separation whereby the sinner is separated "unto obedience and the daily sprinkling of the blood of Christ." It is here that you will get your minds cleared up so as to have a distinct and definite conception before you of the nature of that act of separation which is called by the name of election. It is the separation of a condemned and trembling spirit to the enjoyment of the daily sprinkling of Christ's blood; and so far as this object is to be effected, it cannot be effected save by an act of God, who alone can justify. But justification alone is not election. It is the process of separation whereby an unregenerated soul is brought into a condition of progressive obedience, which shall issue in being presented without blame before God at last; and, so far as this object is to be effected, it can only be effected by being born again, or regenerated by the Spirit of God. But regeneration alone is not election. This process of separation, on the part of God, is a process whereby (the Word of God distinctly informs us) the twofold object of obedience and sprinkling of the blood of Christ is brought about; and, therefore it must, as a matter of necessary consequence, consist in the justification and regeneration of the sinner, viewed, not separately, but in harmonious combination. We have before told you that there is a common principle which all election claims, whether it be angelic or national or sacerdotal or regal or mediatorial or evangelical. The principle which is common to all is that which distinguishes election itself from the purpose to elect; but just as there is a principle of agreement which is *common to them all*, so there must be something in *each which distinguishes it* from all the rest. And here we have, accordingly, discovered wherein the distinguishing feature of evangelical election consists.

It is the process whereby God separates a sinner of the human race from other sinners round about him, and it consists in the twofold act and process of justification and regeneration combined. Both are essential towards the removal of the only hindrances which intercept between any sinner and the subordinate and ultimate objects of election; and, therefore, evangelical election, viewed distinctively from every other election whatever, can consist in nothing more, nothing less, nothing else, than the conjunct removal of the condemnation and the enmity which are peculiar to the unbelieving souls of men.

The conclusion at which we have thus arrived, is confirmed and established from the plainly revealed fact, that the election of which we speak is brought about in every instance THROUGH THE INSTRUMENTALITY OF MEANS.

This is an important truth, which is very clearly revealed to us in the Word of God. In that passage from the second chapter of second Thessalonians, already referred to, the inspired apostle says distinctly, that the elect are chosen to salvation "*through sanctification of the Spirit and belief of the truth.*" What can be more distinct than this? It is not *to* sanctification of the Spirit, but *through* sanctification of the Spirit that the process of election is carried on by God. It is not *to* the belief of the truth, but *through* the belief of the truth that we are chosen to salvation. Such a distinct revelation as this is decisive of the whole question, by which the minds of men have been agitated and convulsed upon the subject of election. The dominant and prevailing theories, the fallacy of which has been already very fully pointed out in previous lectures, are every one of them based upon the erroneous assumption, that the elect have been chosen from eternity *to* the sanctification of the Spirit and belief of the truth. Take away the word *"to"* which is expressive of an end or object to be attained, and substitute in its place the word *"through,"* which is expressive not of the end to be attained, but of the means whereby any object or end is brought about, and you change entirely the whole aspect of the doctrine now under consideration. But who has a right to take away what God himself has introduced, and in its stead to substitute an expression which alters entirely the whole aspect of theology! Who has a right to say that the elect are chosen *to*, when God himself informs us that they are chosen not to but *through* sanctification of the Spirit and belief of the truth? There may be a question started as to the import of the expression, *"from the beginning"* God hath chosen you, but there cannot be any debate about the import of the statement, that it is *"through* the sanctification of the Spirit and belief of the truth" the elect are chosen. Some may argue that the expression "from the beginning" refers us back to eternity, while others may contend that the apostle refers to the beginning of their Christian life—the time when they first believed. We are not careful to interfere at all with this question, seeing that whatever view you take of the expression "from the beginning," the great truth developed in the text remains the same. If you shall decide that the phrase "from the beginning" is expressive of that eternity which preceded all time, you cannot deny the fact that it is plainly declared, that they who are chosen are chosen through means of the sanctification of the Spirit and belief of the truth. And you will not affirm that the elect were actually sanctified by the Spirit, and did actually believe the truth before they came into existence. But you will admit that they could not be actually chosen before it was possible for them to become the subjects of the sanctification of the Spirit and the belief of the truth, for this very obvious reason, that it was through means of these that they were chosen, and their separation or election actually effected. Should you therefore be of opinion that the phrase "from the beginning" is expressive of eternity, you are thereby shut up to the admission that the phrase "*chosen to salvation*" is expressive not of actual election from eternity, but of election in purpose, or God's eternal purpose to elect. But the moment that you are shut up to this admission, you are shut up thereby to an admission of the great truth for which we contend. We contend earnestly for the truth, that whatever God does in time he purposed from eternity to do. But we contend with equal earnestness for the other truth, that election is in no instance a transaction of a bygone eternity, but a transaction of God effected in time; and that it is a transaction effected in time only, after a sinner believes the gospel, is *demonstrated* by the fact, that it is through the means of the sanctification of the Spirit, and the belief of the truth, that any sinner is actually, in point of fact, chosen by God.

You have the same truth brought out by Peter in the verse, from the first chapter of his first epistle, which we have also referred to before. We have already seen from the examination of that verse that the two proximate and subordinate ends which God accomplishes in the election of the sinner, are "obedience and sprinkling of the blood of Jesus Christ." It is TO these ends that sinners are elected. But the verse refers also to the means through which these ends are attained. It is expressly said, "*through sanctification of the Spirit.*" We cannot conceive of any truth more plainly revealed than this, so that if any man shall still deny that election is something which God, in every instance, effects through means, we have a right to hold up these plain statements of Scripture before him, and to charge him with a presumptuous denial of the Word of God. Unless, therefore, a man be prepared to rush heedlessly against the thick bosses of the Almighty's buckler, and to court the awful "WOE" which rests upon "him who striveth with his Maker," and to make the God of truth a liar to his face, we cannot conceive how in the face of these plain Bible announcements, he can persist in holding by the flagrant absurdity of an eternal election, or refuse candidly and honestly to confess that election is a transaction of time, effected by God through means of the sanctification of the Spirit, and the belief of the truth.

It is only upon this principle that it is possible for any man satisfactorily to explain such a passage as the following:—It is written in 2 Peter i. 10, "Wherefore the rather, brethren, give diligence to make your calling and election sure; for if ye do these things, ye shall never fall." Now, on the supposition that election is an act or purpose of the Divine mind formed from eternity, we defy any man to furnish a satisfactory explanation of this verse. On this supposition it would amount to little short of blasphemy to call upon men to make their election sure or firm. How should any creature be called upon to make a decree or act or purpose of the Divine mind sure or firm or steadfast? The conception is blasphemous, and it is nowhere suggested or countenanced in the Scriptures of truth. We are not ignorant of the bungling attempt which is made to explain away this text, and to shade its meaning and eclipse its glory. We are informed, for example, that Peter wanted those Christians to whom he wrote to make *themselves* sure of the reality of their calling and election, and that there was no uncertainty or doubt hanging over the matter save only in their own minds. This explanation is consistent enough with the system of error which it is framed to support, but we appeal to every unprejudiced and honest man if such an explanation be not a barefaced explaining away, an evident perversion, of the inspired words. There is no shade of doubt hanging over the translation of the original Greek. No scholar has ever ventured to propose, and no man can possibly propose a different collocation of the words. The simple term translated sure, means nothing else than sure or firm; and Christians are therefore called upon to make their *calling* and *election* sure. Now, you will notice that the Calvinist does not propose a simple *explanation* of the words,—he proposes a complete alteration of their evident meaning and import. He denies what the words affirm, and he affirms what other passages of Scripture plainly contradict. The words affirm the possibility and the duty of Christians to make their calling and election firm and sure; but the Calvinist finds it necessary to deny the possibility of any man making his calling and election sure, in order to maintain the credit of his soul-deluding divinity. Other passages of Scripture plainly declare, that the believer in Christ, when he is believing, possesses the assurance of his salvation. But the Calvinist chooses to write down a contradiction of this truth, and to insert his falsehood in place of the other truth which the text we are examining evidently contains. This text says nothing at all about assurance of salvation as possessed by believers,—it speaks of the calling and the election of believers, and it contains an exhortation to believers to make their calling and election firm and sure, thereby implying, that it is through the instrumentality of means placed by God at the Christian's disposal, that their calling and election are in point of fact carried into sure and certain execution.

Look at this text in the clear sunlight of revealed truth, and all is beautiful and consistent. Remember that the process of election, or separation of believers unto obedience and sprinkling of the blood of Jesus Christ, is carried on by God through means of the sanctification of the Spirit and belief of the truth; and in the light of this plainly revealed fact, you will at once perceive how believers are called upon most consistently to make their calling and election sure. Let it be remembered that the calling spoken of here, is the calling *to glory*—that calling which is almost exclusively spoken of in the New Testament epistles—that calling which is addressed exclusively to believers. Let it be farther remembered, that this high calling to the future possession of eternal glory, goes hand in hand, and side by side, with the election or separation of the souls of believers from the world around them. The call to eternal glory is ever addressed to them by God while he carries on the process of election or separation of the soul, in all its powers and affections and desires and aspirations, from a wicked and ungodly world. The prize of this high calling is held out to them at the distance, even while God selects or separates them for himself. Now, observe, that the means through which this call to glory is addressed to them, are the same as those whereby they are chosen or elected or separated in their thoughts and feelings and desires and hopes from the vanities of time. It is through sanctification of the Spirit and the belief of the truth that they are both called to glory, and separated unto obedience and the daily sprinkling of the blood of Jesus Christ. Here is their calling and election, which they are exhorted to make firm and sure. Now, how could they do this but by co-operation with God? God it was who addressed to them the call to glory, and sought more and more to elect or separate them from the world through the sanctification of the Spirit and the belief of the truth. But it was their duty to be fellow-workers with God—it was their duty to "work out their sanctification with fear and trembling," not the less diligently that "God wrought in them both to will and to do of his good pleasure." The means whereby God elects or separates were all provided and plied by God. The means for the removal of that condemnation which stood out as the gigantic hindrance to the daily sprinkling of the blood of Jesus Christ—this consisted in the death of Jesus for their sins, and this was provided by God. The means for the removal of that unregenerated mind which stood out as the gigantic barrier to a course of progressively holy obedience—this consisted in the influence of the Holy Spirit, and this also was provided by God. The faith of the truth whereby alone the sinner can possibly enter into union, and retain increased communion with Jesus, and thereby rise from a state of condemnation to a state of justification;—the faith of the same truth whereby alone the sinner can possibly receive the influence of the Spirit, and thereby become the subject of regeneration;—here is another Divinely accredited means whereby the calling and election of any man is exhibited and carried out into practical execution. Here is the connecting medium between the soul of the sinner and the power of God,—the connecting medium between the soul of the sinner and that calling and election of which Peter speaks, and of which the Bible is full. How then is the believer to make his calling and election firm and sure? Clearly by persevering steadfastness in the faith of the truth—by holding fast the beginning of his confidence steadfast unto the end—by a simple, childlike, vigorous reliance on the truth of God, so that faith might grow and flourish and expand and produce fruit in abundance, to the praise and glory of God.

You will see, therefore, how it comes to pass that believers are called upon to make their calling and election firm and sure. They are required to do this because the prize of the high calling at last, and their actual separation unto obedience and the daily sprinkling of the blood of Jesus Christ—their actual separation to progressive holiness here and ultimate glory hereafter, is a process which is carried into effect by God through the instrumentality of means; and the means, so far as man is concerned, is the faith and obedience of the truth. The other means essential to the carrying out of election, or separation from the world, were provided by God independently of, and entirely without the co-operation or consent of men. The sacrifice of Christ has been provided, and the Holy Spirit is provided, and the truth to be believed is provided by God, and placed freely at every sinner's door. All things are ready for the immediate election of the sinner. But inasmuch as man is a free agent, and is graciously furnished with everything necessary to the faith of the truth, it is at this point that he is called upon to act his part, and to give credit to the testimony of the Spirit who speaks to him of Jesus. Inasmuch, therefore, as the faith of the truth is one indispensable means of election, the sinner prevents God from electing or separating him from the world while he refuses to believe. There is no election *out of* Christ. It is *in* Christ, as the apostle, to the Ephesians, declares, that God hath chosen any sinner, or ever will or ever can choose any sinner on the face of the earth. But while the sinner remains unconverted—while he remains an unbeliever, he remains out of Christ, even as the uningrafted branch has no connexion with the vine. But while you admit that the apostle says that believers are chosen *in Christ,* do you ask what is meant by being chosen in Christ *from the foundation of the world?* In this case, I refer you, in one word, to what has been already said. It is election in purpose, or the purpose to elect, which was formed from eternity. This purpose was based upon God's infallible foreknowledge of the undecreed faith of men. Hence Peter says that we are "elect according to the foreknowledge of God." But, as we have already said in previous lectures, foreknowledge fixes nothing—foreknowledge decrees nothing—foreknowledge leaves the sinner as free to act as if nothing were foreknown. But God purposed from eternity to give unto you the power to believe, and he purposed graciously and earnestly to call upon every one of you to believe, and he *foreknew* with unerring certainty every sinner who will listen to his voice, and believe in his Son; and he purposed whenever the sinner believes and is united by faith to Christ to elect or separate that sinner unto obedience, and the daily sprinkling of the blood of Christ on earth, and perfect glory in heaven. The phrase—"chosen in him before the foundation of the world," is exactly parallel to the kindred phrase—"the Lamb slain from the foundation of the world." In both instances, the phrase refers to the purpose of God, and the sinner is not thereby said to have been actually elected before the foundation of the world, any more than Jesus is said to have been actually slain from the foundation of the world. You will observe, therefore, that the great Bible doctrine of election is uniformly consistent with the entire gospel scheme. It hinders no man from salvation. It is the sinner's own unbelief which stands out as the only hindrance. The doctrine of election invites and entreats and opens up the way, so to speak, to every sinner. The means whereby every soul of you may be separated, or chosen, or elected by God, are already provided. *The Son of God has died for your sins.* Here, then, is the only ground of immediate acceptance—the immediate removal of condemnation. Here is the ground on which pardon is freely proclaimed to you all, and on which you may instantly be justified. *The Holy Spirit is present in his blessed influence*, and he knocks at the door of every sinner's heart, seeking this very night admission into the soul. Here is the agent—the blessed agent in regeneration, by whose influence every soul of you may this very evening be regenerated. *The truth of God* respecting Jesus as your Saviour—that truth is before you in the inspired volume, the letter of love from God to man. Here, then, is the means whereby the work of Jesus justifies the soul,—here the means by which the Holy Spirit sanctifies. But if you will not credit it when your Bible tells you that "God is love," and love to you—if you will still hesitate and doubt, and treat God as if he had written down a lie, and sent it down to you in the shape of truth—if you will not believe that God is satisfied by what his Son did for you on the cross, and fancy yourselves not good enough yet to be saved—if you will still persist in seeking some qualification within yourselves, as if God were inviting the righteous and not sinners to repentance—or if ye will remain careless about the revelation of God's love, and count it a small thing to be assured that, for Jesus' sake, every sinner in this house is this moment as welcome to enjoy his Maker's friendship, as if he never had sinned—in one word, if ye will not believe God's truth, but will persist in unbelief, you cannot possibly be elected by God. But the damnation of your souls will lie for ever at your own doors, and your blood will rest eternally and exclusively and justly upon your own heads.

The practical question, after all, resolves itself into

this—Will ye submit your wills unto God's will so as to become partakers of this most blissful and most holy election? There are many who have no objections to be elected to safety and to happiness apart from a life of active, and laborious, and world-forsaking, and self-denying consecration to the service of God and of holiness. Such an election has no existence, save in the depraved imaginations of deluded *Antinomians*. "Be not deceived, God is not mocked. Whatsoever a man soweth, that shall he also reap. He that soweth to the flesh, shall of the flesh reap corruption; but he that soweth to the Spirit, shall of the Spirit reap life everlasting." "Without holiness, no man shall see the Lord." The choice, then, is before you. We dare not bribe you into the church of the living God, by concealing from you the fact, that there is no salvation for any man disconnected from holiness of heart and holiness of life. Be it known unto you, men and brethren, that holiness of heart and holiness of life, is *itself salvation*. It is not the *ground* of salvation. No. *The finished work of Jesus* for your sins; that is the only foundation or ground of any solid hope for time or for eternity. It is not even the *means* of salvation. No.—*Simple faith* in Christ as your Saviour; that is the one only means whereby any soul can possibly come into the possession of the great salvation. But since holiness is not the ground or foundation on which a man may stand and apprehend salvation as all his own; and since it is not even the means through which a man may ultimately reach it, does any man inquire—

What is the use for holiness? Our answer to such an inquirer is—"*Holiness is salvation.*" We do not say, indeed, that holiness is the first or preliminary stage, so to speak, of any man's salvation. We say the very reverse, when we contend earnestly against the universally prevalent delusion, that the sinner must needs be holy *first*, or that the sinner can possibly be holy *first*, before he is in a pardoned state, and in a position to know that he is pardoned and justified and saved from impending wrath. No sinner can possibly enter upon the path of holy obedience, until he knows assuredly that his sins are freely pardoned. Holiness, therefore, is not needed, either to render it consistent with God to pardon your sins, or to assure any sinner that his sins are pardoned. The assurance of pardon must needs precede and anticipate any and every holy emotion within the soul, and any and every holy action in the life; so that if you have never known the blessedness of "the man whose iniquities are pardoned, whose sins are covered, and to whom the Lord imputeth not iniquity,"—which blessedness arises from a conscious sense or assurance of forgiving mercy;—if you are still the subjects of doubts and fears upon this great preliminary step in the experience of every child of God, you need no other or stronger evidence to convince you that you are "still in the gall of bitterness and in the bond of iniquity." But it is equally true, my brother, that if you are assuring your soul of a free forgiveness, and talking of "peace with God," and entertaining the hope of future blessedness, while you still retain the consciousness within your bosom, that (though men who see not into the heart, treat you as one of God's children), you are *not loving Jesus Christ because he has already* saved you from condemnation, and because you know, and rejoice in knowing, that he saves his people, not only from condemnation, but "*from their sins;*"—if having the consciousness of an imaginary justification through his blood, you lack the consciousness of a sincere desire and earnest readiness to sacrifice all that is dear to flesh and blood, in order to be assimilated to his blessed image;—if there is one solitary object on earth, or one solitary lust of the flesh, which you are not ready to sacrifice at the bidding of Jesus Christ;—you may, indeed, pass current among men for a child of God, but in the eye of God, and in the light of God's truth, you stand out *a self-convicted hypocrite.* The sooner you flee to Christ, the better for your poor soul. You are deceiving yourself, if you think you are safe for eternity. You are wilfully shutting your eyes against the salvation of the gospel. You are assuredly turning the grace of God into licentiousness, and making Christ the minister of sin. "If any man come after me, and hate not father and mother, and houses and lands, yea and his own life also, *he cannot be my disciple.*" You must make an absolute and unconditional *surrender* of your own depraved will to God's will, before you are even in a position to apprehend clearly the blessed message which brings to your door a free salvation. You have not yet apprehended the light—the true light shining around you. What is the reason? Why do you not receive Christ's salvation, but choose rather to soothe your soul by a false and presumptuous *assurance of safety?* Yours is not the assurance which the people of God, in every age, have every one of them possessed. Yours is the *assurance of presumption.* It has not led you to surrender *all* to the disposal of your God. There is some favourite idol still within your soul. You may be looking with pity upon those around you who make an idol of a minister, or a church, or a man-made creed, whereby they are prevented from opening their eyes upon the glorious gospel; but "why beholdest thou the mote that is in thy brother's eye, and seest not the beam that is in thine own eye? Thou hypocrite, first cast out the beam that is in thine own eye, and then shalt thou see clearly to cast out the mote that is in thy brother's eye." Thou speakest truly enough when thou sayest that an unscriptural *creed* prevents many from looking at the truth; but this is only one form of the delusion whereby Satan deceives and retains within his grasp the souls of men. What if thy neighbour loves his *creed,* or his religious sect, or party orthodoxy, more than Christ, while you love some other object more than Christ? What that object is, I know not; but *God* knoweth, and *thine own conscience* will reveal it unto thee, if thou wilt but listen to her faithful voice. I again press the question, *Why* do you not receive Christ's salvation? *What is the reason* of your remaining unbelief as to this, while it may be you are consoling yourself under the assurance of a pardon which God has nowhere revealed, and which it is impossible for God to grant to any being in the wide universe—*a pardon disconnected from holiness?* Hear our Saviour's infallible reply: "This is the condemnation, that light has come into the world, and men love the darkness rather than the light *because their deeds are evil.*" John iii. 19. "Their deeds are evil." Such is the reason why they love the darkness and will not open their eyes upon "the true light"—the light which unfolds the salvation of the gospel—the light which shows all who will look upon it, that the salvation of the gospel is a salvation *from all sin* as well as from merited punishment. "Their deeds are evil." Some men see at a glance that if they were to be at peace with God, they would need to part with some questionable or, it may be, positively sinful occupation—others suspect at once that if they were to be friends with God and to enjoy assurance of salvation, they would incur the displeasure and be made the laughing-stock of their unconverted friends. They want a religion which will keep their consciences at ease, while they retain their sinful occupation, or keep up their intercourse with their most agreeable companions, and so they love the darkness—they choose rather to retain a human error which instructs them to suspend assurance upon future procrastinated amendment, and to shut their eyes against the light of gospel truth, which would bring them to immediate and perfect peace, but which would also dissociate them from what they love.

But many more there are whose "deeds are evil," and they would retain their sins and be excused from "*denying themselves and taking up their cross;*" and so they separate in their minds between safety and holy living, and they shut their eyes against the light which reveals *the only pardon* of the gospel — the pardon with self-denial, and active, laborious, flesh-crucifying, and world-sacrificing holiness, beneath and behind it. And so they learn to speak of peace with God and assurance of a possessed and enjoyed salvation—deceiving and being deceived! The last error is worse—infinitely worse, because more dangerous, than the first. We would not therefore deceive you. We would rather inform you plainly, that unless you have made up your minds to sacrifice whatever you may discover to be inconsistent with the will of God, and to do whatever God shall require you to do, though it should be at much painful cost and sacrifice to flesh and blood, you cannot possibly be Christ's disciples. There is a free pardon for every soul of you in Christ, and that even now. But the enjoyment of this gracious forgiveness is only preliminary to a life of progressive holiness on earth, and an eternity of holiness beyond the grave. It is for you, beloved friends, to make your choice. I know full well that, at this moment, every feeling of your souls, and every association of your thoughts, and every habit of your lives, and every impulse of your desires, and, it may be, every apparent temporal interest with which you are bound up, chime in with the syren song of a false and destructive orthodoxy, which bears onward impetuously against the truth of God, inducing you to close your eyes against the light of life, and your understandings against the candid and serious examination of the gospel of salvation. Of this I am not ignorant; but you are not left without an opposing influence which would lead you to Jesus, and to true and lasting happiness. And with this better influence bearing upon your minds, and soliciting your instant decision on the side of God, you have the power to resist all that infernal influence whereby you are led astray, and this instant to choose "the good part which shall never be taken from you." God the Father pleads with you; God the Son pleads with you; God the Spirit pleads with you. The interests of eternity are set against the selfish and mistaken interests of time; and you are asked by God himself to say, "What is a man profited, though he gain the whole world and lose his own soul?" And you have the power to decide for God and for happiness in opposition to every allurement which seeks to enchant you, and which beckons you downward to destruction. You have the power to will or to choose the good rather than the evil, even now while the current of evil is bearing you impetuously along on its dark and troubled bosom. You have not yet reached the farthest verge over which many a deluded soul is carried, and plunged into the deep unfathomable abyss beneath, from which there is no escape. You have the power to choose, as we have endeavoured in former addresses to demonstrate in your hearing. It is for you to consider the freeness of that salvation which is announced to you, and to look well at its nature as a salvation from condemnation this very moment, in order to subsequent and entire consecration of all that you are, and all that you have, to the service of your God. You have the power to make it this very moment entirely and everlastingly your own, in fullest and most blissful possession; but you have the power to decide against it and to rush upon perdition. There cannot be any other alternative; FOR it or AGAINST it, you must this night, every soul of you decide. Hesitancy and doubt, and procrastination till some more convenient season—these are present determinations of your will *against* salvation. Before you is the blessing and the curse!—both are before you. The claims of God and the sinful allurements of the flesh! —both are before you. An open heaven and a gaping hell!—both are before you. Heavenly truth exhibited by the Holy Spirit as the guide-mark to glory, and hellish error exhibited by Satan, in the shape of an angel of light, to allure you to everlasting woe!—both are before you. No power in the universe can constrain your choice. God himself cannot FORCE you to choose—the decision is in your own hands. "*Choose ye* this day whom ye will serve. If *Jehovah* be God, serve him; but if *Baal* be God, serve him."

APPENDIX.

We have quoted, in pages 100 and 112, from the work of Zanchius in defence of Calvinism, translated by Toplady, in order to establish what many blind and ignorant Calvinists of the present day endeavour to deny—the identity of Calvinism with the FATALISM of the ancients. We here subjoin what Toplady himself published, and what the late Dr. Pringle of Perth republished, in the way, not of DENYING (for it cannot truthfully be denied), but of explaining and defending, after pleading guilty to the charge. Our readers will be pleased to mark the absence of all reference to the Word of God, and the barefaced appeal made by CHRISTIAN MEN to HEATHEN AND ANTICHRISTIAN PHILOSOPHERS in support of this theology! If the supporters of this system could discover in *the Bible* any foundation for their creed, would they be foolish enough to make their appeal to a document like the following? But we cheerfully give them the benefit of the *best defence* of their system they can find, and here append the entire document. It is intituled

AN APPENDIX concerning the FATE OF THE ANCIENTS. From the Latin of JUSTUS LIPSIUS.*

Fate [says Apuleius] according to Plato, is that, "Per quod, inevitabiles cogitationes Dei atque incepta complentur;" *whereby the purposes and designs of God are accomplished.* Hence, the Platonics considered *Providence* under a threefold distinction: 1 The *Providentia prima*, or that which gave birth to all effects· and is defined by them to be, *του πρωτου Θεου νοεσις, the intention* or *will of the Supreme* GOD. 2. The *Providentia secunda*, or actual

* Vide LIPSII Physiolog. Stoic. Lib. 1. Dissert. xii.

agency of the secondary or inferior beings, who were supposed to pervade the heavens, and, from thence, by their influence, to regulate and dispose of all sublunary things; and, especially, to prevent the extinction of any one *species* below. 3. The *Providentia tertia*, supposed to be exerted by the *Genii;* whose office it was, to exercise a particular care over mankind: to *guard* our persons, and *direct* our actions.

But the STOICAL view of Providence, or Fate, was abundantly more simple, and required no such nicety of distinction. These philosophers did, at once, derive all the *chain of causes and effects* from their true and undoubted *source*, the WILL of the ONE LIVING AND TRUE GOD. Hence, with these Sages, the words DEITY, FATE, PROVIDENCE, were frequently *reciprocated* as terms synonymous. Thus Seneca, speaking of God; "Will you call him *Fate?* You will call him rightly: for all things are suspended on him. Himself is *causa causarum*, the cause of causes beside." The laws of the universe are from God; whence the same philosopher, elsewhere, observes, "Omnia certa et in æternum dicta lege decurrere:" *All things go on, according to a certain rule or decree ordained for ever:* meaning in the law of Fate. So Cicero: "All things come to pass, according *to the sovereignty of the eternal law.*" And Pindar, probably, had an eye to this, where he says, Νομον παντων Βασιλεα, Θανατων τε και αθανατων, ειναι. That *The law ruleth all, whether gods or mortals.* Manlius most certainly had:

Sed nihil in tota magis est mirabile mole.

Quam RATIO *et certes quod* LEGIBUS *omnia parent.* Where by *Ratio*, is evidently meant, the *decreeing mind* of God; and by *Leges*, is meant *Fate*, or that series of causes and effects which is the offspring of his decree.

Homer cannot begin his Iliad, without asserting this grand truth: Διος δ' ετελειετο βελη: *the counsel* or *decree of Jupiter was fulfilled.* The divine poet sets out on this exalted principle; he puts it in the front of the noblest poem in the world, as a testimony both of his *wisdom* and his *faith.* It was as if he had said, "I shall sing of numberless events, equally grand, entertaining and important; but I cannot begin to unfold them without laying down THIS, as a first, fundamental *axiom*, That, though brought to pass by the instrumental agency of men, they were the fruit of God's determining Will, and of his all-directing Providence."

Neither are those *minuter* events, which seemingly are the result of *chance*, excluded from this law: even these do not *happen*, but *come to pass* in a regular order of succession, and at their due period of time. "Causa pendet ex causa: privata ac publica longus ordo rerum trahit," says Seneca: "Cause proceeds from cause: the long train of things draws with it all events, both public and private." Excellent is that of Sophocles; (*Aj. Flagell.*)

> *Εγω μεν ουν και ταυτα, και τα ταντ' αει,*
> *Φασκοιμ' αν ανθρωποισι μηχαναν Θεους.*
> *'Οτω δει μη το δ' εστιν εν γνωμη φιλα,*
> *Κεινος εκεινα στεργετω· καγω ταδε.*

i. e. "I am firmly of opinion, that all these things, and whatever else befall us, are in consequence of the Divine purpose: whoso thinks otherwise, is at liberty to follow his own judgment; but this will ever be mine."

The *Longus ordo rerum*, mentioned by Seneca, is what he elsewhere styles, "*Causarum implex series*," or a perpetual implication of causes. This, according to Laertius, was called by the Stoics, *αιτια των οντων ειρομενη*, an involved, or concatenate causality of whatever has any existence: for, *ειρμος* is a chain, or implicate connexion. Agreeably to this idea, Chrysippus gives the following definition of Fate: *'Ειμαρμενην ειναι, φυσικην συνταξιν των ὁλων εξ αιδιου, των 'ετερων τοις 'ετεροις επακαλουθουντων, αμεταβολου και απαραβατου ουσης της τοιαυτης συμπλοκης.* "Fate is that natural, established order and constitution of all things, from everlasting, whereby they mutually follow upon each other, in consequence of an immutable and perpetual complication."

Let us examine this celebrated definition of Fate. 1. He calls it a natural *συνταξις*: meaning by nature, the great *Natura Prima*, or GOD: for, by some Stoics, GOD and NATURE are used promiscuously. But, because the Deity must be supposed both to *decree* and to *act* with *wisdom*, *intelligence*, and *design*, FATE is sometimes mentioned by them under the name of *λογος*, or *Reason*. Thus they define FATE (*Laert.* in *Zen.*) *'ειμαρμενεν, λογου, καθ' ὁν ὁκοσμος διεξαγεται*, to be that supreme "Reason, whereby the world is governed and directed;" or, more minutely thus, *λογον, καθ' ὁν στα μεν γεγονοτα γεγονε, τα δε λεγομενα γινεται, τα δε γενησομενα γενησεται*: "that reason, whereby things that have been, were: the things that now are, have a present existence: and the things that are to be, shall be. *Reason*, you see, or *Wisdom*, in the DEITY, is an antecedent cause, from whence both *Providence* and inferior *Nature* are derived. It is added in *Stobæus*, *μεταλαμβανει δε του λογου, την αληθειαν, την αιτιαν, την φυσιν, την αναγκην*, i. e. that Chrysippus sometimes *varies his terms*; and, instead of the word *reason*, substitutes the words *truth*, *cause*, *nature*, *necessity*; intimating, that Fate is the true, natural, necessary cause of the things that are, and of the manner in which they are.—2. This FATE is said to be *εξ αιδιου from everlasting*. Nor improperly: since the constitution of things was settled and fixed in the Divine mind (where they had a sort of ideal existence) previous to their actual creation: and therefore, considered as certainly future *in his decree*, may be said to have been, in some sense, co-eternal with himself.—3. The *immutable and perpetual complication*, mentioned in the definition, means no more than that reciprocal involution of causes and effects, *positis omnibus ponendis*, are necessarily produced, according to the plan which infinite wisdom designed from the beginning. GOD, the First Cause, hath given being and activity to an immense number of *secondary*, subaltern causes; which are so inseparably linked and interwoven with their respective effects (a connexion truly admirable, and not to be comprehended by man in his present state), that those things which do in reality come to pass *necessarily*, and by *inevitable destiny;* seem, to the superficial observer, to come to pass in the common course of nature, or by virtue of human reasoning and freedom. This is that inscrutable method of Divine wisdom, "A qua" (says St. Austin) "est omnis modus, omnis species, omnis ordo, mensura, numerus, pondus; a qua sunt semina formarum, formæ seminum, motus feminum atque formarum."

NECESSITY is the consequence of *Fate.* So TRISMEGISTUS: *Παντα δε γιγνεται φυσει και ʽειμαρμενη, και ουκ εστι τοπος ερημος προνοιας, προνοια δε εστι, αυτοτελης λογος του επουρανιου Θεου. Δυο δε τουτου αυτο φυεις δυναμεις αναγκη και ʽειμαρμενη*: i. e. "All things are brought about by Nature and by Fate; neither is any place void of Providence. Now, Providence is the self-perfect reason of the supercelestial God; from which reason of his, issue two native powers, Necessity and Fate." Thus, in the judgment of the wiser heathens, *effects* were to be traced up to their producing *causes;* those producing causes were to be farther traced up to the still *higher causes* by which *they* were produced; and those higher causes to GOD, the cause of them. *Persons, things, circumstances, events,* and *consequences* are the effects of *necessity;* Necessity is the daughter of *Fate:* Fate is the offspring of God's infinite *wisdom* and sovereign WILL. Thus, all things are ultimately resolved into their Great Primary Cause; *by* whom the chain was originally let down from heaven, and *on* whom every link depends.

It must be owned, that *all* the fatalists of antiquity (particularly among the Stoics) did not constantly express themselves with due precision. A Christian, who is savingly taught by the Word and Spirit of God, must be pained and disgusted, not to say, shocked, when he reads such an assertion as *Την πεπρμενην μοιραν αδυνατον εστι αποφυγειν και Θεω. God himself cannot possibly avoid his destiny* (Herodot. 1.), or that of the poet Philemon:

> *δουλοι βασιλεων εισιν, ʽοι βασιλεις Θεων,*
> *ʼΟ Θεος αναγκης.*

Common men are servants to kings; kings are servants to the gods; and God is a servant to necessity. So Seneca: "Eadem necessitas et Deos alligat: irrevocabilis Divina pariter atque humana cursus vehit. Ille ipse, omnium conditor ac rector, scripsit quidem Fata, sed sequitur. Semper paret: Semel jussit." "The self-same necessity binds the gods themselves. All things, divine as well as human, are carried forward by one identical and overpowering rapidity. The supreme Author and Governor of the universe hath, indeed, written and ordained the Fates; but, having once ordained them, he ever after obeys them. He commanded them at first, for once: but his conformity to them is perpetual." This is, without doubt, very irreverently, and very incautiously expressed—whence it has been common with many Christian writers, to tax the Stoics with setting up a First Cause superior to God himself, and on which he is dependent.

But, I apprehend, these philosophers meant, in reality, no such thing. All they designed to inculcate was, that *the* WILL *of God and his Decrees are unchangeable:* that there can be no *alteration* in the *Divine intention;* no *new act* arise in his MIND; no reversion of his eternal *plan;* all being *founded* in adorable *Sovereignty;* ordered by infallible *Wisdom; ratified* by *Omnipotence;* and *cemented* with *Immutability.* Thus Lucan:

Finxit in æternum causas; qua cuncta coercet,
Se quoque lege tenens.

And this, not through any *imbecility* in God, or as if he was *subject* to Fate, of which (on the contrary) himself was the *ordainer;* but because it is *his pleasure* to abide by his own decree. For, as Seneca observes, "Imminutio majestatis sit, et confessio erroris, mutanda fecisse. Necesse est ei eadem placere, cui nisi optima placere non possunt:" "It would detract from the greatness of God, and look as if he acknowledged himself liable to mistakes, was he to make changeable decrees: his pleasure must necessarily be always the same; seeing, that only which is best can at any time please an all-perfect being. A good man (adds this philosopher) is under a kind of *pleasing* necessity to do good; and, if he did not do it, he could not be a good man."

"Magnum hoc argumentum est firmæ voluntatis, ne mutare quidem posse:" "It is a striking proof of a magnanimous will, to be absolutely incapable of changing." And such is the will of God—it never fluctuates nor varies. But, on the other hand, was he susceptible of change; could he, through the intervention of any inferior cause, or by some untoward combination of external circumstances, be induced to *recede* from his purpose and *alter* his plan; it would be a most incontestable mark of *weakness* and *dependence:* the force of which argument made Seneca, though a heathen, cry out, "Non externa Deos cogunt; sed sua illis in legem æterna voluntas est:" "Outward things cannot compel the gods; but their own eternal will is a law to themselves." It may be observed, that this seems to infer, as if the Deity was still under some kind of *restraint*. By no means. Let Seneca obviate this cavil, as he effectually does, in these admirable words: "Nec Deus ab hoc minus liber aut potens est; IPSE ENIM EST NECESSITAS SUA:" "God is not hereby, either less free or less powerful; FOR HE HIMSELF IS HIS OWN NECESSITY."

On the whole, it is evident, that when the Stoics speak, even in the strongest terms, of the *obligation* of *Fate* on *God himself*, they may, and ought to be understood, in a sense worthy of the Adorable Uncreated Majesty. In thus interpreting the doctrine of Fate, as taught by the genuine philosophers of *the Portico,* I have the great St. Austin on my side: who, after canvassing and justly rejecting the bastard, or *astrological Fate*, thus goes on: "At qui omnium connectionem seriemque causarum, qua fit omne quod fit, *Fati* nomine appellant; non multum cum eis, de verbi controversia, certandum atque laborandum est: quandoquidem ipsum causarum ordinem, et quandam connectionem, SUMMI DEI tribuunt VOLUNTATI:" i. e. "But for those philosophers [meaning the STOICS] who, by the word Fate, mean that regular chain and series of causes to which all things that come to pass owe their immediate existence; we will not earnestly contend with these persons, about a mere term: and we the rather acquiesce in their manner of expression, because they carefully ascribe this fixed succession of things, and this mutual concatenation of causes and effects, to the WILL of the SUPREME GOD." Austin adds many observations of the same import, and proves, from Seneca himself, as rigid a *Stoic* as any, that this was the doctrine and the meaning of his philosophic brethren.

THE END.

www.ingramcontent.com/pod-product-compliance
Lightning Source LLC
LaVergne TN
LVHW010219110826
845151LV00004B/1140